C000091757

Developing Yourself and Your Staff

M. NASIR SAMAD
TEL: 087 - 2341656
NCIR '98

THOROGOOD

THE PUBLISHING
BUSINESS OF THE
HAWKSMERE GROUP

Published by Thorogood Limited
12-18 Grosvenor Gardens
London SW1W 0DH.

Thorogood Limited is part of the
Hawksmere Group of Companies.

A CIP catalogue record for this Pocketbook is available from the British Library.

ISBN 1 85418 069 X

Printed in Great Britain by Ashford Colour Press.

Designed and typeset by Paul Wallis at Thorogood.

Front cover: © Bridgeman Art Library
– *Perpetual Motion* by Rene Magritte.

Business Action Pocketbooks

Business Action Pocketbooks are concise but comprehensive reference books designed to fit in your pocket or briefcase to be a ready source of business information. Each *Pocketbook* gives an introductory overview of a single topic and is followed by around 20 sections describing a particular aspect of that topic in more detail.

Pocketbooks will be of use to anyone involved in business. For owner managers and for managers in bigger businesses they will provide an introduction to the topic; for people already familiar with the topic they provide a ready reminder of key requirements. Each section concludes with a checklist of useful tips.

This book is based on *Business Information Factsheets* researched and written by enterprise and economic development agency, Project North East. Section contributors include Linda Jameson, Andrew Maville and Bill Waugh all of whom work at PNE. The series has been edited by David Irwin.

The information is checked by an independent expert to ensure, as far as possible, that it is accurate and up to date. However, neither the publishers nor the authors can accept any responsibility for any actions that you should take based on its contents. If you are in doubt about a proposed course of action, you should seek further professional advice.

Other titles in the 'Pocketbook' series

Business Action Pocketbooks are a series of concise but comprehensive reference books. Each one contains sections describing particular aspects of a topic in detail and checklists with useful tips.

Building Your Business

This *Pocketbook* provides practical information about growth, strategy and business planning. Effective leadership, problem solving, decision making and the formal aspects of running a business are also covered in this guide which will help to define your strategy and ensure that you achieve your stake in the future.

Managing and Employing People

Discover the key to successful people management by motivating, stimulating and rewarding your staff.

Practical information and advice about recruiting staff, employee rights and obligations, effectively managing people and the legal aspects of employment are all covered in this *Pocketbook*.

Finance and Profitability

Practical tips and techniques for profitable management, including costing and budgeting, record keeping and using financial statements and understanding and finding investment are given in this *Pocketbook*. There is also advice on financial forecasting, monitoring performance against your plans and retaining effective financial control. This book will help ensure that your business is successful and profitable.

Sales and Marketing

This *Pocketbook* is an excellent reference tool focusing on the overall process of sales and marketing. It will help give you a direction and a set of goals along with practical tips and techniques for successful market research, segmentation and planning, promoting, selling and exporting. It will help you take those first important steps towards establishing a presence in your market.

Contents

Introduction

Introduction

The importance of people

To manage your business effectively you must manage two elements: people and processes. The greater of the two is people. It makes sense doesn't it? All businesses are dependent on people – on their skills, experience, motivation and morale.

If the people are right and the processes wrong, people can make the processes right. You might ask what if the processes are right and the people wrong? That is unlikely, because if the processes are working well, the people must be too.

One important way to stimulate staff to perform well is to offer a programme of continuing professional development, stimulating and challenging them to achieve more in their work, but backing that up with opportunities for training and personal development.

From vision …

Not surprisingly, if training is going to be effective from the business's point of view, it has to reinforce the business's objectives. Furthermore, the day to day objectives of the business have to help it progress towards achieving its strategic objectives. In turn, those objectives have to be defined in terms of work tasks. Satisfactory completion of tasks, of course, require that members of staff are assigned to those tasks, with specific personal objectives. Objectives and tasks should be agreed regularly between you and your staff.

... *to development needs*

There are, effectively, three ways in which a business identifies development needs.

Firstly, they will arise from strategic decisions. The decision to introduce ISO 9000 for example requires not only a training programme to introduce all staff to the requirements of TQM and ISO 9000, but also a need to have internal auditors. You might address this need by training staff, or you could buy in an internal audit service.

Secondly, development needs will arise from operational objectives. The decision to offer NVQs as part of your management training programmes, for example, may require assessors and verifiers. You could buy them in or you could choose to become an approved delivery centre, training your own staff to provide those functions.

The business's goals, strategic objectives, operational objectives and project tasks can then be summarised in a table, as shown over, together with the identified development requirements.

Organisation development plan

Strategic objectives	Goals	Operational objectives	Project tasks	Development req's
Develop new markets through joint ventures	Establish international joint venture	Identify suitable partner Prepare business plan and financial forecasts	Identify suitable products Identify appropriate markets Prepare detailed costings	Understand local legal requirements Learn foreign language
Improve means of storing and retrieving information throughout company through use of information technology	Establish intranet linking all staff and all offices	Install computer network Identify revised staffing needs Train staff	Install network Recruit additional staff Set up staff training programme Transfer existing systems Set up for use as intranet	Expertise in network administration Programming using HTML languages All staff to understand how to maximise benefit from system
Continuously improve effectiveness of staff	Achieve recognition as an Investor in People	Introduce continuing professional development	Revise appraisal system to reflect requirements of CPD Introduce personal development logs	Train line managers in appraisal skills

As far as organisational development is concerned requirements may be addressed in a number of ways, perhaps by buying in equipment, or by buying in a service, or by recruiting staff with appropriate skills, or by training existing members of staff.

For activities to be accomplished, of course, requires people to be allocated to tasks. In some cases, the allocation of a project task and a personal development need to go hand in hand.

There is a third way in which development needs arise. That is where members of staff and/or their line managers identify weaknesses or development needs relating to the way those staff are carrying out current activities and where they are forecasting likely activities, say 6 - 18 months ahead, which may require training or personal development in advance.

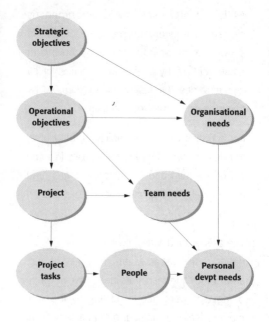

It is important therefore, for all members of staff to set out and agree both short and medium term targets and objectives and to link a personal development plan to those objectives. In the normal course of events medium term objectives will become short term objectives – though medium term objectives may require a short term development plan.

To capture everyone's personal development plan and to demonstrate a plan's relevance to your business's objectives you may find it helpful to set out personal development plans as part of the appraisal process, perhaps including relevant boxes on the form that you use, such as those illustrated below.

Personal development plan

Organisational objectives	Personal development plan	
	Objectives	Review
Short term (0-6 months)		
Complete preparation of IT strategy	Be able to reconfigure computer network to use Windows NT	February
Install network	Be able to provide appropriate support to rest of staff	April
Set up staff training programme		
Transfer existing systems	Be able to manage additional staff	April
	Understand requirements of HTML and to be able to use MS Front Page and MS Internet Explorer	February January
Medium term (6-12 months)		
Set up network for use as intranet		

If this is done properly, it should ensure that every member of staff:

- Has clear work objectives

- Can see how their job is likely to develop

- Understands what development work is required to help achieve their work objectives, and,

- Undertakes training that is relevant to their job and avoids participating in programmes just for the sake of it.

For most people, development is likely to come about through:

- Work based, on the job, instruction and work experience, and

- Participation in formal training courses.

Although less likely to be immediately relevant to specified development objectives, professional development will also come about through:

- Informal activities including reading of relevant books, professional journals, etc

- Researching academic papers, preparation of training materials, writing books etc and

- Attendance at (appropriate) conferences, meetings of professional institutions, etc.

All of these activities should be recorded perhaps in a 'personal training record' which will provide a permanent record for the member of staff – and, more importantly, a reminder which can act as the basis for a review of effectiveness at the next appraisal.

A personal training record

Development objective: to be able to reconfigure computer network to use Windows NT and to provide appropriate support to rest of staff			
Date	Activity	Type	Duration	Confirmed by
2-5/12	Training course provided by MARI	T	28	CW
Dec	On the job – introducing Windows NT and resolving problems	W	5	CW
Jan	Reading Microsoft manual and using TechNotes	I	4	

T: Participation in formal training courses **W:** Work based training **I:** Informal personal development
R: Research **C:** Attendance at conferences, etc.

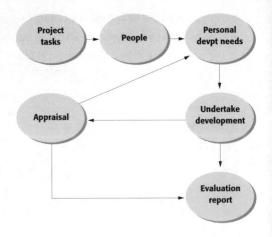

Reviewing effectiveness…

It is essential to review effectiveness at the end of each training programme. For example, ask staff to complete a simple evaluation form to assist you to assess the immediate value of specific training inputs.

At the person's next appraisal, review progress made towards achieving the development objectives and review how the training has improved the person's ability to contribute to their work. Has the person put into effect what they have learned? Has their behaviour changed?

The appraisal interview also provides an opportunity to review individual tasks and development objectives and to review and update the personal development plan.

… and economy

You will naturally be concerned about the cost of training and whether you are getting value for money. Ideally, you need to determine whether the cost of the training (in fees and staff time) is more than covered by the benefits (in improved effectiveness, productivity, efficiency, etc). Where the development is the acquisition of a practical skill it is relatively easy to measure benefits and effectiveness. For development needs which are more subjective, evaluation may depend on a combination of factors which include assessment by the individual and the stakeholders in that individual development. Stakeholders may include the appraiser, the project manager, external customers of the project or task etc.

The learning process

Whilst we may not recognise it, most of us are learning all the time. We take in news on television and radio and if we are particularly struck by a story we will listen carefully to find out what is happening. At work, in most organisations there are fewer instances of demarcation of tasks then ever before. Most people now are expected to be multi-skilled, as well as being able to juggle a number of activities at once. This means that learning is a continuous process, which we often undertake unwittingly. If, however, you understand the learning process it is likely that both you and your staff will be able to learn faster.

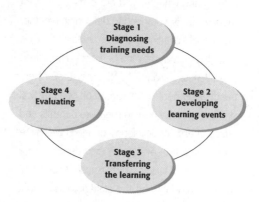

Diagnosing training needs

The first stage is the diagnosis of a training need. There are many indicators which can demonstrate the need for training: you might find recurring faults; one person may repeatedly ask questions about their work; you may receive complaints from customers; perhaps you have introduced new equipment; you may have identified training needs during an appraisal or you may just realise that some people could be helped to work more effectively. The best way to diagnose the nature of training required is to undertake a training needs analysis. The theory behind TNA is that to do any task well you need the relevant knowledge, skills and attitudes. Knowledge can be classified as the information to do the task, skills are the abilities to do the task and attitudes are the feelings necessary to perform a task effectively. Development might be needed in any of these areas and the nature of the need may dictate the nature of the training.

If, for example, you wanted to assess whether your existing receptionist needed any additional training, you would consider the tasks to be undertaken and then decide what knowledge, skills and attitude were desirable in order to complete the tasks.

Example

Receptionist's tasks:

- Use telephone system, fax and copying machine.

- Advise visitors of availability of staff.

- Word process documents.

- Make tea and coffee.

- Take messages.

The desirable knowledge, skills and attitudes to undertake these tasks are shown in the table overleaf.

Receptionist: desirable attributes

Knowledge		Skills		Attitude	
Company background	Health and safety rules	Communication	Switchboard	Self-motivated	Encouraging
Organisational structure	Customer information	Interpersonal	Listening	Pleasant	Helpful
Use of communication system	Internal procedures	Telephone	Questioning	Patience	Flexible
Switchboard	Computer use	Decision making	Fax machine /photocopier	Tolerance	Products service
Who's who	Functions of organisation	Presentation	Writing	Responsive to needs	Awareness of own role
Staff movements	Who's who at clients	Dress sense	Typing/computing	Customer awareness	Vigilant
		Interaction	Shorthand	Attitude to customers	Thorough
		Customer care	Organisational		Approachable
		Customer awareness	Coffee making		

The knowledge, skills and attitudes must also be measurable to be able to identify where training needs lie and to what extent. For example, the receptionist must have knowledge of the company's products, but does she simply need to know their names or must she also know how to assemble them?

One way of assessing the current level of capability is to use a 'skills appraisal card'. Activities are listed in order of importance and employees must assess which skill level they have reached on each activity.

Skills appraisal card

SALLY SMITH (RECEPTIONIST)	CAN TRAIN OTHERS	HIGH SKILL LEVEL	MEDIUM SKILL LEVEL	LOW SKILL LEVEL
Knowledge of company products and services	✔			
Knowledge of customers	✔			
Knowledge of competitors		✔		
Word processing skills			✔	
Ability to do shorthand				✔
Ability to use switchboard			✔	
Use of fax machine	✔			
Use of photocopier				

Another option is the 'skills appraisal table' which allows you to assess the current level of competence against that required. From this it is possible to see where the greatest training needs lie. Any minus values in the 'total' column indicate a training development requirement.

*(See the 'skills appraisal table' for **Receptionist Sally Smith** overleaf)*.

Assessment of an employee should involve both the employee and the manager in order to get a good indication of the employee's capabilities.

In a small business it is a good idea to undertake skills appraisal with every person to ensure that they are working effectively. If your resources are limited it is important that you are confident everyone in your business is contributing to their full potential.

Developing learning events

Once you have identified the needs for development in your business it is important to act upon them. There are many types of learning events, and each individual need will dictate the type of learning event most appropriate. It is usual that improvements to performance can be most influenced from within the organisation as the

Skills appraisal table for Sally Smith

KNOWLEDGE, SKILLS AND ATTITUDE	ACTUAL LEVEL	REQUIRED LEVEL	TOTAL
Knowledge of company's products and services	6	8	-2
Knowledge of customers	9	7	+2
Knowledge of customers	5	5	0
Ability to communicate well	8	10	-2
Ability to use the telephone system	10	10	0
Word processing skills	5	8	-3

ownership of the method and process will be internal. Specific new skills may need external training programmes.

Learning events

Method	Advantages	Disadvantages
Job shadowing	Easily related, low cost	Pick up other's mistakes
External courses	More intensive	Expensive
Distance learning	Learn at own pace	Need self-discipline
Open University	Learn at own pace	Need self-discipline
Night classes	Better concentration on topic	Not always appropriate
Day release	Better concentration on topic, interaction with others	Expensive
Learning by mistakes	Concrete learning experience	Can be expensive
Customer complaints	Easily related	Can demotivate
In-house training	Inexpensive	Possible personality clashes
Secondment	Can set strict objectives, avoid company politics	Must benefit employee and organisation
Videos	Convenient to use	Not always relevant
Audio cassettes	Convenient to use	Not always relevant

Method	Advantages	Disadvantages
Software packages	Uniformity of training, can be used repeatedly	Low feedback
Books	Inexpensive	Need self-discipline
Research projects	Self directed	Need self-discipline
Outward bound courses	Team building, confidence building	Expensive
Role play	Need real experience	Can be uncomfortable
Mentoring	Build strong relationship	What are benefits to mentor?
Workshop	Can be done in-house or externally, shared experiences	Not specific
NVQs	Meets specified standards	Time consuming, expensive
Apprenticeship	High skill level achieved	Time consuming
Experience	Good learning opportunities	Mistakes can be costly
Teamworking	Interaction and learning from others	May not be sufficiently rigorous

Transferring the learning

The third stage in the learning process is transferring the learning. Once the training needs have been identified and possible learning events have been assessed, it is important to ensure that the learning 'sticks'. This means that the learning is remembered after the learning event.

You may decide that you will take a member of staff out with you to visit clients for a day, in order that enquiries will be dealt with more effectively in the office in future. You need to communicate the relevance of what you will both do and why. Do not forget the objectives of the learning event. You must also ensure that the staff member gets an opportunity to use their new knowledge promptly afterwards, so before your day out agree action to be undertaken in the weeks following it.

You must also check for feedback after the event to ensure that facts have been understood.

An effective way to plan learning will include these steps:

- Agree an action plan.

- Give a full brief prior to the learning event so that staff understand what they will be doing and, more importantly, why.

- Use a news reporter style – tell them what you are going to tell them, tell them and then tell them what you've told them!

- Feedback – clarify that everything has been understood correctly.

- Use a selection of training aids and tools.

Evaluating the learning

This is the final stage in the learning process. Evaluation is important to ensure that the training needs analysis was accurate, that learning has been successful and that any necessary modifications are identified. Evaluation must encourage the learner to express honestly their opinions or views. So, if you are using a questionnaire to evaluate the learning process, wording must be carefully considered. Evaluation should involve assessment of the immediate benefits gained by the learner, but also the long term effect the training has had on the organisation as a whole.

Team building

1 Approaches to team building

This section looks at a number of ways to understand and develop teamworking in the business.

Introduction

A team approach can be used to solve particular problems, or as the entire basis for running a business. People can, however, be cynical about working in a team. Their experience is all too often of factionalism and conflict. To work properly, teams must be properly selected, given time to develop, and be well led.

Teamworking is not an exact science. Individuals and situations vary too much for there to be hard and fast rules. The following section discusses a number of ideas that have proved helpful in developing productive teams. You will modify these ideas in the light of your own experience. The essential thing is to understand the value of a team approach and to have a commitment to making your teams work more effectively.

Why build teams?

It is increasingly recognised that businesses are more effective when they involve their employees in the management and development of processes. The business benefits from a wider pool of knowledge and experience and employees act more responsibly and are more motivated in their work.

Benefits of team building:

Innovation

a) Teams create a good environment for the discussion of problems, new ideas, and improved work methods.

b) Teamworking stimulates creative thought and the cross fertilisation of ideas leading to more innovation.

c) A team approach leads to quicker implementation of new ideas making the company more adaptable and flexible.

Staff development

a) General motivation and job satisfaction are improved.

b) Staff become more adept at handling conflict. Problems can be resolved through discussion before they get out of hand.

c) Members of a team understand what is expected of them and can monitor their performance. This makes performance feedback more meaningful.

d) Individuals feel encouraged to try new ideas and test their abilities. Individual skills and abilities are developed and put to more effective use.

Effectiveness and efficiency

a) Staff involvement in planning leads to goals that are more realistic and achievable.

b) Teamworking can bring everybody together, staff and management, engendering a greater sense of loyalty and a common commitment to success.

c) Staff from different departments get the chance to work together, discuss issues and solve problems.

d) Employees become more supportive at work. They are in a better position to assist when problems arise.

e) Members conform their behaviour to meet team standards. This can encourage more disciplined work habits without a feeling of compulsion.

Characteristics of teams

In life we find ourselves involved in a variety of groups (eg family, friends, departments, etc). A team is where the group is formed to achieve a common purpose. The more effectively they work together, the better the team. A good way to understand the qualities that make good teams is to compare them with groups.

Problems that can occur in groups

a) People work independently and often at cross purposes.

b) Suggestions are not encouraged. People are told what to do, or wait to be told.

c) People play games instead of working together, eg members are cautious about what they say, so it can be difficult to understand what they mean.

d) Members are not adequately involved in planning the group's objectives and focus mainly on their own interests.

e) Members may have valuable expertise to give, but domineering members deliberately restrict their contribution.

f) Motives are not trusted because roles are not understood. Opinion or criticism is not encouraged and is seen as being non-supportive.

g) Conformity is valued more than good results.

h) Tensions build up and individuals find themselves in conflicts that they are unable to resolve. Supervisors may not intervene until it is too late.

i) Members do not participate in decisions affecting the team. They do not feel personally responsible for success or failure.

Features of a good team

a) Members recognise their dependence on one another and realise that supporting each other is the best way to achieve personal and team goals. They do not waste time seeking personal gain at the expense of others.

b) Members try to understand each other and make an effort to practise open and honest communication.

c) Members realise that conflict is unavoidable. They try to resolve conflicts quickly and also recognise the opportunity for new ideas to emerge.

d) Members are committed to the goals that they helped establish. They feel a sense of ownership for their unit and their job.

e) Positive results are the goal.

f) Members trust each other. Questions are welcomed. They feel free to express their disagreements, opinions and ideas.

g) Members realise that in an emergency or when agreement cannot be reached, the leader must make the final decision.

h) Members help achieve success by applying their own knowledge and special talents to the objectives.

i) Members receive support from the team and are encouraged to develop skills and apply what they learn on the job.

Methods for developing teams

Teams take time to develop. There are many different theories concerning the evolution of teams but most of them follow similar patterns.

Charles Handy has identified four stages of team development:

a) Forming – members are still a collection of individuals who are just beginning to form a single identity.

b) Storming – there is conflict. People are 'feeling' each other out. Attitudes are displayed. Boundaries are set.

c) Norming – trust begins to develop and the team begins to work together.

d) Performing – the team begins to perform at its best.

Handy has identified three elements which affect the outcome of successful team building:

a) The group

b) The task

c) The environment. The process of interaction, the process of decision-making, maintenance functions, and leadership style are other intervening factors.

Kiddy and Co identified the main five elements for successful team building:

a) Manage the task. Use systematic working methods such as planning, objective setting, managing time, etc to complete the job.

b) Manage the process. Use interpersonal skills such as listening, encouraging, and summarising to help people contribute to their fullest potential.

c) Manage communications and competition. Use political as well as negotiating skills to reduce the harmful effects of intergroup competition between different work groups and disciplines.

d) Management style. Change management behaviour as needed to fit the needs of the situation.

e) Manage contributions. Understand that people are different and learn how to use these differences most effectively.

Good communication is essential for the effective team

The TORI model was developed by Pfeiffer. He suggests four main factors which foster open communication:

a) Trust – members must have confidence in each others abilities and attitudes.

b) Openness – a free flow of information, ideas, perceptions and feelings must exist between members. This process involves self-disclosure.

c) Realisation – members must possess self determination and have role freedom.

d) Inter-dependence – members must feel a sense of shared responsibility and must have some influence over one another. There should be a shared vision of a common future.

The 'Ashridge Team-Working Approach'

This aims to provide a common language of teamworking, comprehensive enough to cover the complexities of how a team works, yet simple enough to remember. Eight basic concepts help identify strategies and skills that work and contribute to success. Shared standards and values characterise the team's vision and provide a systematic approach to analysing performance. Further details in *Superteams* by Hastings, Bixby and Chaudhry-Lawton.

Team building cannot happen overnight. It is a continual process that requires a lot of feedback and review. Factors that affect the team are constantly changing. The team must be aware of these changes and know how to react accordingly.

Forming successful teams

When selecting, it helps to choose members with specialist knowledge as well as team working ability. A successful team consists of members with a variety of personality types and strengths.

Team roles

Belbin has identified eight different roles that he found present in successful teams.

a) Company worker – practical organiser, worker.

b) Chairman – co-ordinates effort, social leader, does not have to be brilliant.

c) Shaper – task leader, dominant, outgoing.

d) Plant – ideas person, creative, intelligent.

e) Resource investigator – diplomat, Mr Fix-it, salesman, popular.

f) Monitor-evaluator – analytical rather than creative.

g) Team worker – mediator, uncompetitive, supportive.

h) Completer-finisher – worries about deadlines, checks details.

In his book *Management Teams* Belbin describes these characteristics in greater detail.

Suggestions to forming successful teams:

a) Identify areas where the team is lacking in knowledge, resources and experience.

b) List the areas of expertise your team needs to be successful.

c) Have team members brainstorm and compile a list of people that could be of assistance in different areas. Give a copy of this list to all team members.

d) Identify who will be affected by the team's actions. Allocate responsibility for developing each of these relationships. Pay particular attention to those who feel threatened by what the team is doing.

e) Ask people outside the team what they believe the strengths and weaknesses of the team are.

f) Explain to the organisation why the team was formed, what they will be doing, etc.

g) Publicise the team's success.

h) Avoid stereotyping, generalisations and off-loading blame.

i) Match the attributes of members and the responsibilities of the team.

Teams with more than 11 members tend to be ineffective. Studies show that teams are most effective when they consist of between six and eight members.

Leadership

Leadership skills can be developed, but they also depend greatly upon individual personality. You must be confident, mature and assured in a position of leadership, but not so powerful as to undermine the confidence of others.

Features of a good team leader:

a) Must be able to get people involved and make them feel committed.

b) Allows people to perform and makes it easy to see the opportunities available for teamwork.

c) Lets team members be responsible for solving problems.

d) Monitors conflict and intervenes before it becomes destructive.

e) Visionary about what people can achieve as a team.

f) Keeps to commitments and expects others to do the same.

g) Inspires teamwork and mutual support as well as stimulating excitement and action.

h) Proactive in relationships.

i) Looks for people with the desire to excel and to work constructively with others.

j) Encourages questions and fosters open discussion.

k) Co-ordinates the team effort.

l) Develops a reward system that satisfies the needs of the team as well as the individual needs of the members.

m) Encourages new ideas and experimentation.

Leading teams to success:

a) Provide feedback to the team and be open to receiving it yourself.

b) Mutually set goals with team members and discuss expectations.

c) Allow team members to be involved in any activity that they can make a contribution to.

d) Be aware of the team's progress. Recognise and reward the team and its members accordingly.

e) Do not allow competition and conflict to reach the point where it will cause damage, but recognise that some conflict is unavoidable.

f) Understand how teams work and get practical experience of forming, developing and leading them.

- *A wide range of team building courses are available. Some of the most effective of these are held in residential outdoor centres. This can provide a stimulating environment to test out your leadership qualities, and to put theory into practice.*

- *Encourage activities (eg team sports after work) which nurture team building. Test out teamworking approaches in non-critical areas before you introduce them more widely.*

- *If you are not genuinely committed to a team approach, token team building activities will be counter productive.*

- *Look for employees who can work in teams and be prepared to remove those who cannot.*

2 **Staff development methods**

This section summarises the main areas to be considered when developing staff.

Introduction

By adopting a systematic approach to staff development, employers can encourage staff to maximise their contribution at work and can ensure that the necessary skills are available to meet business objectives. Staff development is therefore a continuous process which promotes the efficient utilisation of human resources and can be a powerful motivator of employees at all levels.

Staff development policy

Training and development plans are often seen as 'flavour of the month' activities, particularly if top level support is absent. Managers should therefore be closely identified with staff development if success is to follow.

This is often best achieved through a formal staff development policy agreed by senior management and circulated to all staff. The policy statement should include a statement of intent and then should set out company wide development policies and indicate the strategies to be employed to meet those objectives. The statement may also indicate relationships between development plans for individuals and those for departments. Links with succession planning and equal opportunities policies are stressed in many development policies.

Through the 'Investors in People' (IiP) initiative introduced in 1992, organisations can gain recognition for their commitment to staff development. Achieving IIP is now recognised as the best route to ensuring an effective approach to training and development within a company. The initiative is co-ordinated by local Training and Enterprise Councils (LECs in Scotland) from whom further information is available.

Assessing training and development needs

Over 70 per cent of employers in the UK claim to use a formal method of identifying training needs. These include staff appraisal, assessment of performance against objectives, development meetings and reference to job descriptions.

A systematic development process could include any or all of these approaches but is likely to be based upon business objectives and should involve discussion between managers and their staff. Information useful to development planning is likely to be obtained from the following sources:

- Business plan (including SWOT analysis).

- Departmental objectives and strategies.

- Employee records (past development plans, training undertaken, posts held, qualifications).

- Appraisal system.

- Discussion between managers and staff.

- Analysis of the external environment.

Development needs may be assessed internally or may require the assistance of a training consultant. Many TEC/LEC offices can offer help with assessment and can, in certain circumstances, assist in meeting the costs of training needs analysis consultancy.

Preparing plans

Commitment will normally be increased if staff at all levels are encouraged to participate in preparing development plans for their own sections or departments. If, however, staff are unaccustomed to a development orientated culture it may be necessary to involve a 'change agent' from a consultancy or agency to provide impartial reinforcement.

Supervisors or managers should be made responsible for preparing staff development plans for their own sections. These should evolve through discussions with all staff and with reference to the information sources listed above. Departmental plans can then be summarised in an overall staff development plan for the organisation. By participating fully in this process, employees will understand the reasons why they are expected to undertake development activities. Involvement may lead to raised expectations, therefore development plans should be realistic with regard to budgets and timescales.

Plans for individuals should outline personal development objectives, training development activities to be undertaken, a timescale for their completion and the signatures of the individuals and managers who have agreed to the plan. Copies of the plan should be retained by the individual, his/her manager and the personnel section (if the organisation is large). If several objectives are identified it is important to establish which have priority.

Monitoring

It is normally the responsibility of managers to ensure that development plans for their staff are carried out. In larger organisations, the Personnel Department may also have a monitoring role. Committed employees would also be expected to take responsibility for their own development and draw managers' attention to any developments that may arise.

Whenever a development plan is prepared a review date will normally be set. The review could take place as part of an appraisal interview but many employees prefer to separate performance appraisal from staff development and therefore have distinct meetings for each purpose.

Staff development records

Staff development records are an integral part of personnel record keeping and can be maintained within a manual or computerised system.

A record for each member of staff will normally contain details of existing qualifications, development plans, current development/ training activities and any special skills which could in future be useful to the organisation. A section for notes/comments may also be provided.

Computerised personnel record systems, which are widely available for use on micro-computers, normally include a format to record staff development. A simple database for this purpose could however be easily set up on any business computer.

Methods of development

In-company

a) On-the-job-training

The most common form of employee training is on-the-job-training. This method involves little cost and avoids any need to release staff to attend training elsewhere. Without careful planning and monitoring, however, on-the-job-training can be ineffective, with inadequate or no learning objectives and a danger of bad habits being acquired.

Planned experience alongside a skilled operator can form a valuable part of staff development but may need to be supplemented by some formal input to ensure that both understanding and skills are developed. Assessment against objectives can support this process.

b) Competence based training

At national level competence based training is becoming widespread. This approach concentrates upon accrediting performance against the key competences (or abilities) required to perform a particular job. Accreditation takes the form of a National Vocational Qualification (NVQ) or a credit toward an NVQ.

Competence based training is currently being developed across a wide range of occupational areas from operator to management levels. Competences must be assessed by a qualified assessor, usually from a college or training consultancy. Some, usually large, firms have however obtained training for one or more of their staff to become qualified assessors. Most competence based training and assessment takes place on-the-job. Some formal, off-the-job training is usually required, therefore release of staff may be necessary. Due to the time involved in assessment, competence based training is not a cheap option.

c) Developmental placement

A business which has several departments or functional areas can broaden staff skills and experience via placements in different departments. Placements which involve real responsibility can heighten appreciation of the business as a whole and can bring fresh ideas to the 'host' department. A placement without clear responsibility and measurable objectives can, however, demotivate both the individual and the department.

In very small organisations, internal developmental placements may be impractical but secondment to other organisations could be considered, perhaps with the help of the TEC/LEC or Enterprise Agency.

d) Open/flexible learning

This approach avoids the financial and practical implications of releasing staff for training and instead relies upon materials which staff can study at home or in time allocated at work. Flexible learning is often popular among staff who are reluctant to re-enter formal education but can prove difficult unless support is available from in-company or external sources. The benefits of flexible learning can be maximised by establishing in-company support groups of staff pursuing similar courses.

External

Training and development obtained from external sources has traditionally been divided into short practical courses and longer, usually certified, education courses. This distinction is becoming increasingly inappropriate as many short courses gain NVQ recognition and longer courses are converted into modular programmes which are compatible with competence based training.

It is therefore possible for employers to build training programmes from a variety of sources to meet the exact needs of their staff. Short, formal modules, can be obtained externally to supplement work-based training/experience, then the resulting package can be presented for external accreditation by an award making body.

This may also involve the accreditation of prior learning (APL) undertaken by the member of staff. Decisions about particular development and training opportunities should therefore include the potential for a qualification to be gained. Advice about the availability of particular qualifications via competence based training, APL and Credit Accumulation and Transfer (CATS) can be obtained from local colleges and universities. The availability of the above routes to qualifications has, in some cases, led less established training consultants to offer cut price deals to employers, thereby undercutting existing providers. It is wise to check the background and status of any consultant before agreeing a contract for services of this type.

Measuring the benefits

Few small businesses attempt to measure the benefits of their investment in training. Without such evaluation it is difficult to justify further investment.

Evaluation can be against skill criteria, productivity objectives or other targets depending upon the level and nature of work involved. Short-term improvements may also be noticeable in absenteeism and other morale related measures.

Paying for staff development

Staff development can appear an expensive activity, particularly when the costs of releasing staff are added to course fees and examination/accreditation fees. Several sources of assistance are available to help employers meet these costs:

- Local TECs/LECs offer a variety of grants and incentives to encourage staff training and are particularly keen to fund multi-employer and innovative training programmes. Other sources of grant funding include local authorities and the European Community.

- Training for employees up to 18 years of age is normally funded through Youth Training, co-ordinated by TECs/LECs. The scheme is applicable to young people in employment as well as those placed with YT agents.

- Individual employees can apply for Career Development Loans to fund training/ development which will assist their own careers. Interest on these loans is subsidised by the government and repayment is delayed until training is completed. Details are available from high street banks.

- Some tax relief is now available for individuals undertaking vocational training. See Inland Revenue leaflet IR 119 or contact your nearest Revenue office for details.

- *Make clear your commitment to development for yourself, your managers and your staff.*

- *Plan staff development to meet current and future business needs.*

- *Measure the benefits of all development activities and training programmes.*

- *Use free information available from TECs/LECs, educational institutes and Chambers of Commerce.*

Personal development

part
two

3 Negotiating skills

This section explains the key principles of the art of negotiating.

Introduction

An owner-manager of a small business whether buying, selling or discussing employees' wages, must get the best possible deal without creating unnecessary conflict. Negotiations should be collaborative and constructive, satisfying both parties. If one party 'wins' at the other's expense, this may jeopardise further business opportunities. However, there will, almost certainly, be occasions when you will find yourself in competitive negotiations. Negotiation skills can be learned and improved through practice.

Important principles

Negotiating may be visualised as the process of finding the point of balance between your own objectives and the objectives of the other party. Negotiations can be 'competitive' or 'collaborative'. In competitive negotiations the negotiator wants to 'win' even if this results in the other party 'losing'. It often ends in confrontation. In collaborative negotiating an agreement is sought which is satisfactory to both parties, ie to maximise mutual advantage.

There is no one way to negotiate. Each person will develop a style which suits them. Your skills will develop with experience. You can also learn how to negotiate from books and short training seminars. To negotiate successfully it is necessary to learn how to:

- Understand the importance of preparation

- Understand how to develop objectives for negotiations

- Understand the strategies, tactics and signals which may be used and,

- Assess realistically the chances of successful outcomes in negotiations.

Negotiating stages

There are five essential stages in the negotiating process:

Prepare

a) Define your objectives

These must be specific, achievable, and measurable. In other words, you must have a clear idea of what you want from the other party, you must be realistic and you must be able to assess how well you have done. Write them down.

Objectives should also be prioritised. One way to do this is to classify them as 'must achieve', 'intend to achieve' and 'like to achieve'. For example, you have bought a photocopier for your office. It breaks down after a week and you have to contact the supplier. What are your objectives?

Must achieve: the use of a photocopier that works.

Intend to achieve: get your photocopier repaired.

Like to achieve: get a replacement photocopier.

b) Research

Gather as much information as possible about the subject to be negotiated. The person with the most information usually does better in negotiations. For example, two chefs are each preparing a very important meal. They both need a lemon but there is only one lemon in the kitchen, so the chefs argue over who needs the lemon most. They could cut the lemon in half but they both need a whole lemon. Consequently, both would 'lose' or the senior chef could pull rank, resulting in the junior chef being the 'loser', the result being the possible loss of his future co-operation. If they had initially obtained more information they would have found out that one chef required the juice of the lemon and the other chef the rind. A 'win/win' situation could have been achieved.

Discuss

This is the process of exploring each party's needs, starting with tentative opening offers. These need to be realistic, otherwise there will be little scope for a satisfactory conclusion. If both parties are co-operative, progress can be made. If one side is competitive, problems may arise. Analyse the other party's reaction to what you say.

Use an opening statement covering the main issues at stake for each party. Allow the discussion to develop naturally. Make it clear that at this stage you just wish to talk, not negotiate as yet. Establish a relationship with the other person. Ask questions to find out more about their needs and to keep things moving. The more you find out about one another's needs, the greater the possibility that you will find a mutually acceptable solution.

Propose

This is the stage where you are giving and receiving proposals and suggestions. Remember to trade things, not just to concede them. You'll find this phrase invaluable:

'If you (give us something), then we'll (give you something).'

Look for the opportunity to trade things which are cheap for you to give (but valuable to the other party) in return for things which are valuable to you. For example, Kevin is a painter and decorator who has recently separated from his wife and needs to rent a reasonably priced flat. Mr Smith is the landlord of a property which he is letting for £50 per week. The property is in a relatively bad condition:

Mr Smith: 'The room is £50 per week.'

Kevin: 'That's a little more than I was expecting to pay.'

Mr. Smith: 'There are lots of other people interested in the flat if you don't want it.'

Kevin: 'If you give me the flat for £40 per week, then I'll paint the walls in the living room for you.'

Mr. Smith: 'If you paint the living room and the kitchen then I'll let you have the room for £40.'

Kevin: 'That's a deal.'

Bargain

After discussing each other's requirements and exchanging information, the bargaining can start. Generally speaking, you receive more if you ask for more. If conflict arises at this point, indicate that your opening offer is not necessarily what you will finally accept.

When your offer is made, state this clearly. If you use words like 'approximately' or 'about', an experienced negotiator can challenge on a number of issues and change your offer dramatically.

When the offer has been made, the next step is to find out exactly what it includes. Ask for clarification. You will have prepared a list of your requirements in the preparation stage, so ensure that these are met.

Agreement

When agreement is in sight, listen for verbal indications such as 'maybe' or 'perhaps'. Look for non-verbal signs, for example, papers being tidied away. It is time to summarise what has been discussed and agreed. Do not start bargaining again.

Offer a summary of what has been agreed, this will give a chance to confirm any decisions. As soon as possible after the negotiation send a letter documenting the agreement. Having the agreement in writing is better than a handshake on the deal.

The letter should mention the following points:

a) The terms of the agreement.

b) The names of those involved.

c) The prices mentioned plus discounts etc.

d) Individual responsibilities.

e) Time schedules and any deadlines agreed.

Two approaches to negotiating

Styles of negotiating need to vary according to the circumstances and the people involved. Most negotiations will be a mixture of the collaborative and competitive approaches. On the whole, it is more productive to do what you can to steer proceedings towards collaboration rather than competition.

Competitive

In the competitive approach, negotiations have an unfriendly atmosphere and each party is clearly out to get the maximum for themselves.

Opening: avoid making the opening bid; it gives a great deal of information to the other party. If you encounter a competitive situation you should limit information given and attempt to control the agenda.

Concessions: conceding in a competitive situation is seen as a sign of weakness, so keep it to a minimum. The size of your first concession gives the opposing party an idea of your next best alternative, telling them exactly how far they can go.

Conflict: when conflict comes out into the open, use the skills of assertiveness to maintain your position and defuse the situation. Tactics can include the following:

a) Make sure your position is strong and clear. Prepare well so that your arguments are well supported and to the point. The more relevant information you have the more effective your argument. Irrelevant arguments indicate weakness.

b) Avoid attacking or threatening your opponent. Such behaviour may work in the short term but to an experienced negotiator will indicate weakness. It can imply desperation and the lack of an adequate alternative. Remember your objectives: must, intend and like to achieve.

c) Work on the other party's real needs rather than their expressed desires. Information about this can be obtained from your research, listening skills and by observing body language. For example, an employee may be pushing hard for a pay rise to compensate for the fact that they feel overloaded with work. Focus on the source of the problem, and discuss solutions (eg more forward planning, recruiting an assistant etc).

Collaborative

Negotiation is often seen as a battle where the stronger party defeats the weaker party ie 'win/lose'. In some cases negotiations can break down altogether (eg in an industrial dispute which results in industrial action). Nobody wins ie 'lose/lose'. The collaborative approach is not based on conflict, but upon the belief by everyone involved that it is possible to reach a solution where everyone benefits, ie 'win/win'. This approach tends to produce the best results, mainly because there is much better communication between the parties. In addition, it makes for better long term relations if it is necessary to work together over a long period.

Opening: the opening will involve you gathering as much information as possible but also disclosing information so solutions can be developed that are acceptable to both parties. This can involve:

a) Considering many alternatives for each issue.

b) Using open questions.

c) Helping the other party to expand his/her ideas about solutions.

Concessions: both parties will concede things if necessary. Try to trade things which are cheap for you to give but valuable to the opposing party, in return for things which are valuable to you.

Conflict: if you listen, summarise, paraphrase and disclose (for example, 'I would like to ask you a question…' or 'I feel that I need to tell you that…') in collaborative negotiations, conflict will be kept to a minimum, enabling mutual advantage to be obtained.

USEFUL TIPS

- *Be assertive*
- *Be patient*
- *Be open minded*
- *Display good listening skills*
- *Be self disciplined*
- *Plan carefully and fully*
- *Be creative*
- *Be flexible*
- *Be persuasive*
- *Be decisive*
- *Show confidence*
- *Show consideration.*

4 Assertiveness skills

This section looks at how assertiveness skills can be used to improve working relations.

Introduction

Assertiveness is about reducing and managing conflict, not about creating it. The most difficult part of management can be dealing with people – they can act unpredictably especially in time of stress or disagreement. Managers who assert themselves effectively with employees, colleagues, suppliers and customers, will get better results, save time and be less stressed. Assertiveness helps to provide solutions to difficult situations and to reach constructive compromises that suit everyone. Knowing how to do this well is an important management skill.

What is assertiveness?

Assertiveness is about honestly expressing feelings and needs. Assertiveness allows people to relate to one another in an open and frank way, whilst respecting each other's views and opinions. The aim is to get relationships out of the emotive modes of aggression and passivity, onto a rational level. Focus discussion on the problem, not on the personalities involved.

Constructive solutions can then be found which take account of everyone's needs and wants.

Assertiveness is not to be confused with aggression. Aggressive behaviour ignores the feelings and opinions of others and violates their rights. Aggression may seem to release tension, induce a sense of power, solve problems quickly and earn the respect of others. In the long term it creates an atmosphere of tension and resentment. If staff feel intimidated, they are less effective, withhold information, become demoralised and in some cases, may even leave.

Passive or 'non assertive' behaviour is not standing up for yourself or expressing your views inadequately, if at all. Conflict is avoided, decisions are delayed, self-esteem is low, there is frustration and loss of respect from colleagues. Passivity results from being afraid of the consequences of getting into trouble. Passive people often think they are just being polite or helpful.

Why be assertive?

Handling conflict – assertiveness helps to diffuse difficult situations where people are angry or upset. Conflicts can be resolved and effective solutions found.

Staff development – assertive relations with staff take account of their feelings and views. This helps them work more effectively, and encourages them to make a greater contribution in terms of new ideas and improvements to current practices.

Customer relations – dealing assertively with customers involves being honest about what can be achieved and not making promises that can't be kept.

Communications and teamwork – when everyone in an organisation feels comfortable about expressing their views, communication is improved and people are more likely to say what they really think. Everyone is more aware of where problems lie, and is happier about suggesting solutions and working together to implement them.

Confidence – assertive people are more decisive. Knowing that a situation was handled well improves confidence. Worry and stress are reduced and more gets done. Time management improves. Employees are happier working for someone who is comfortable in a leadership role, and this also affects the attitude of suppliers, bankers, etc.

Negotiating skills – being assertive and confident helps people to get better outcomes from negotiations of all kinds.

Rights and responsibilities

When people are intimidated or bullied, they often feel that their feelings do not matter, that they are getting things out of proportion and deserve to be pushed around. The concept of rights enables someone to judge whether they are being fairly treated, and gives them the confidence to take the appropriate action. Rights are defined as 'something to which you are entitled'. Everybody has certain basic rights. Write down the rights you think people might expect from others in the course of a normal working day. If they are entitled to those rights, then so are you! Here is a suggested list.

- The right to say what you really think.

- The right to a fair hearing.

- The right to be different, to be an individual.

- The right to be treated with respect (eg to be asked, not told).

- The right to say 'no'.

- The right to make mistakes.

If rights are fully accepted, then it will be easier to defend them. With rights come responsibilities, for example, people have the right occasionally to make mistakes – but there is also a responsibility to acknowledge it and to take action. You are also responsible for respecting the rights of others.

Assertive thinking

Positive mental attitude

Many people are defeated before they start because they don't believe that they can succeed. This affects the way they use assertiveness methods, and influences the way they behave when trying to apply them. If you believe you can't do something, you won't. If you believe you can, you probably will – and even if you don't get it completely right, you will probably achieve at least some of your objectives. Beliefs affect behaviour. Whilst you can't change things overnight, getting into the habit of thinking positively about future outcomes will improve your confidence. To make assertiveness work you must believe that you can be assertive and that others are prepared to relate to you on that basis.

Anticipation

For assertiveness to be effective it is important to plan carefully what you want to say beforehand. It is particularly important to be positive immediately before dealing with difficult situations. Take a deep breath, imagine yourself dealing with the situation well and responding assertively. Have confidence in your method. This will improve your performance.

Assertive communication

The aim of assertive communication is to reach a solution that is acceptable to all involved. This can be achieved by a simple three stage process:

- Hear and acknowledge the other person's point of view (eg 'I understand that this new deadline is important');

- State your own views, feelings and opinions (eg 'However, I already have other important tasks to complete at the same time');

- Agree a way forward that is acceptable to both parties (eg 'Why don't we contact the customers involved, explain the situation and find out which work must be done immediately? We can then prioritise the workload and perhaps get some extra help if needed.').

Further assertiveness techniques

Saying 'no'

Many passive people are afraid to say 'no'. However if you cannot possibly do something it is much better to be honest and say so, rather than being polite. This can stop tensions developing and help focus on finding effective solutions.

Empathising

Empathy is when you put yourself in someone else's shoes. Combine empathy with stating your needs. For example 'I know you're really busy at the moment, but…'

Clarification

This is used when you think that what was agreed and what is currently happening are different. For example, 'I understood we were going to do it this way, but now I think you want it done that way; am I correct?' You may want to clarify a task or role assigned. If the discrepancy is deliberate, being assertive will have confirmed that the agreement originally made still stands, or that circumstances have changed – either way, doubt has been removed.

Stating the consequences

This should only be used as a last resort. This approach warns people of the consequences, but also gives options for the behaviour to change (eg 'If this happens again, I will have to apply the formal disciplinary procedure.'). Consequence assertion must only be used when you are prepared to use the appropriate sanctions.

Asking questions

The aim is to discover other's wants and needs by asking clear and direct questions, eg 'Is this the only problem you are having?', or 'So, are you telling me that the new system is in fact giving you more work?'. It is useful when people are being indirect. You can find out exactly where they stand. It can be used to establish whether a certain action is acceptable, to collect information and to check if the other person has the same understanding. It encourages others to express themselves assertively.

Repetition

When negotiating or in discussion, repetition can be very effective. Do not simply repeat your point – this will be dull. Restating your case, in different ways, ensures that your point is made and that the other person has listened and understood it.

Putting assertiveness into practice

Using assertiveness to deal with conflict

If you can maintain a calm, assertive approach when faced with aggression, the other person usually calms down and behaves more rationally. Do not deal with really difficult situations at once. Arrange a later meeting so that everyone can calm down, and you have time to consider what you will say. There are several methods for dealing with aggression. A very effective way is to agree with people who are angry, for example, saying 'Yes, I can see that you are very upset about this'. You have not conceded anything, but have acknowledged their feelings. This should slow them down, and should allow you to go on to explain your views calmly. It is also useful when you are pounced on by an aggrieved person to ask clear and direct questions. Instead of reacting defensively, asking questions gives you information, time to think, time for the other person to calm down and prevents you from taking a hurried decision.

Leadership

Respect the rights of employees, and encourage them to be assertive too. At the same time, employees expect leadership. It is important to be able to assert your authority with confidence. If one person is allowed to get away with things, or to push someone around, others will become demoralised and even disruptive. Surprisingly, you also have to be firm if you wish to praise an employee without embarrassment. Giving employees constructive feedback based on facts and evidence, rather than opinions and qualitative judgements, is easier if employees are treated assertively. Assertive teams communicate and work together more effectively and rationally, and will be able to resolve conflicts quickly and satisfactorily.

Stress

Calmness is crucial. It cools things down and helps you think rationally. Much conflict results from a build up of stress and is often a way to let off steam. Assert yourself when people are less likely to be under stress. Do not react immediately if things are getting on top of you. Give yourself a cooling off period. Finally, before you assert yourself, take a deep breath and try to relax; this will help you think and act more rationally.

USEFUL TIPS

- *Assertiveness methods are not suitable for every situation and some conflicts can't be avoided.*

- *Be natural. It takes time to learn about assertiveness and how to use it. Incorporate assertiveness techniques into your management style and do not expect your behaviour to change overnight.*

- *Don't be put off by failure. Take a long term view, stay positive and learn from your mistakes.*

- *Go on an assertiveness training course.*

5 Time management

This section outlines the principles and methods of time management.

Introduction

Every day we are faced with a host of minor decisions such as, 'What shall I do today?', 'How shall I organise my correspondence?' or 'How shall I approach this next phone call?'. Such things are straight forward in every-day life, but with the multiplicity of tasks and time scales involved in running a business, they become suddenly a lot more complex.

Time management is about developing an organisational system to cope with day-to-day work. Different people and different businesses require different systems (and this should be borne in mind when assessing the relevance of these ideas for particular situations). Much of it may seem obvious, but bear in mind that without some kind of system, the chances of success are known to decrease dramatically.

Plan ahead – make a list

The basic principle behind time management is to get into the habit of setting aside time to think and plan before you take action. People often feel uncomfortable about looking ahead, and instinctively want to 'get stuck in' right away. It can take a long time to learn that a little time invested at the beginning of a task often shortens the overall time taken because you foresee mistakes and identify the quickest way forward. Occasionally, planning may reveal that the task is not worth doing at all. For the owner-manager, such things can be the difference between making a profit or a loss.

It's no use gazing into space – that's prevarication. Always think things through on paper. Most frequently this simply means making a list at the start of every day.

Make your list work

A common mistake is to write out everything you can think of (showing what a hard working person you are) ending up with a massive list which you then proceed to ignore. You must learn how to make the list work for you:

- Make priorities. Mark tasks which are vital A, important B and not so important C. Mark the 'As' 1, 2, 3, etc thus identifying the most important tasks for successful results. Concentrate on getting tasks done in this priority order; tick them off when done.

- Schedule your work. Decide when you will do things and in what order. Block out time for important tasks. Number items where the sequence is important, or where one thing depends upon the other.

- Set a deadline to finish. Deadlines should be tight enough to keep things moving without being unrealistic. If in doubt make it as soon as possible.

You will develop a layout for your own 'To Do' list that suits you. A frequently used method is to divide the list down the middle and use one side to chart out a schedule for the day. This is useful to programme in appointments, and to block out time for major tasks. There should also be space to mark your priorities and deadlines. It should be a handy size so that you can take it with you wherever you go during the day.

Long-term planning

You also need to take time out at regular intervals to look further ahead. This helps co-ordinate workloads and avoid bottlenecks in the long run. Also, if you know that time is reserved to think long-term, it stops you worrying about such issues on a day-to-day basis.

- Weekly planning. On Mondays reserve an hour at the start of the day to look at your long-term plans, your diary and plan the week in view. On Fridays take an hour to think about next week.

- Longer term planning will depend upon your own particular business. Many businesses need monthly planning sessions, especially if they do many one-off jobs and have to juggle workloads around frequently. The same principles for managing the list apply, but a different format might be appropriate. Sessions should ideally incorporate some kind of a review of how things have gone since the previous plan was made.

Whatever 'time-horizons' you work to, it is essential to set aside time every 6-12 months to think about the 'big picture'; is the business achieving its objectives; do you need to change direction?

Keep a diary

A diary is essential equipment for any business. Consult the diary when making appointments, and always mark them in. Tasks to be performed on specific dates can also be marked in; there is no reason why specific periods of time should not be kept free to perform a particular task.

Diaries can also contain general information which can be useful to have at hand, such as telephone numbers. They also act as a history of appointments, events, etc.

Get into good habits

Routines are useful to get things going, get things done, and make the planning process work:

a) Mornings. Look at the plan for the week and your diary and plan the day ahead. Clear the desk and think again.

b) End of the day. Clear the desk and think about tomorrow – it helps in the morning if you started your list the previous day.

c) Friday afternoons are a good time to catch up with filing and deal with trivia.

People function differently at different times of the day. Most people find it is better to do the difficult things in the morning and the easier or routine things in the afternoon. If you have a major problem to solve, tackle it at the time of day when you are at your best, and find a refuge where you can give it all your attention without interruption.

Learn to guard time from others; don't respond instantly when people ask you for things, but programme your response into your future schedule; learn how to say 'no' politely to time-wasters.

Prevarication is a great time-waster. You will only learn to use your own judgement by acting on it. Once you have made your decision, take immediate action. Don't waste time on second thoughts. Make it a point of honour to see the thing through to the end, and to beat your own deadline. A major cause of prevarication can be fear of conflict. Learn the skills of assertiveness and you will hesitate less often.

Try not to put down a piece of paper until it has been dealt with.

Organise information

Don't get swamped in paperwork. A well thought out system will leave the mind free to think business. Here are some ideas:

- Looseleaf file for plans/ideas.

- Concertina file for correspondence (remember to keep a copy of the letters you send too).

- A-Z filing system for information, documents, etc. This can range from a box of folders to a proper filing cabinet.

- A-Z book or card index for names and numbers and addresses.

- Desk trays marked according to urgency (A,B,C) clear desk of excess paperwork regularly.

- Keep a 'C' drawer in your desk for trivia to be dealt with once a month.

- Noticeboard – useful for memos, frequently used telephone numbers, planning charts, etc.

Telephone tips

The telephone is a notorious time waster if it is not used properly. Here are some basic tips:

- List key points to be made (not word for word) to avoid muddle.

- Don't explain too much; get straight to the point (if they need to know more, they'll ask).

- Don't use clever words, keep it simple. It will be understood and people won't think they are dealing with a con-man.

- Take your time. If you rush things you will end up wasting more time repeating yourself, or sorting out misunderstandings.

- Group similar calls to save time.

- Appointments; if unable to reach someone, get a time and call them back (people rarely call back when they say they will – this can waste a lot of time).

- Don't prevaricate. If you have a difficult call to make, and you have done your preparation, pick up the phone and dial!

USEFUL TIPS

- *Be positive. Many people approach time management in the belief that it will not work – with the inevitable consequences. It is important to convince yourself of the value of your own time. A good way to do this is to make a record of how you spent your time in the course of a week. Going back over the record can be a salutary lesson, and make you a far more 'time conscious' person. Once you value your own time, you will find ways of saving it.*

- *Be realistic about what you can achieve. Time management is fundamentally about changing the way you behave from moment to moment. This is hard and should be attempted in realistic stages. People often try too much too soon because secretly they want to prove that it does not work. Also, don't go over the top – you could get over stressed, and worst of all become a real time management bore!*

● *You may be able to go on a short seminar about time management for the owner manager.*

● *You can buy complete self-organising systems such as Filofax. Electronic systems are also available, as is relevant computer software, eg Lotus Organiser. These are very popular, but too many people still don't use these systems to manage their time. Acquire the basic good habits of time management before you decide which system would best suit your needs.*

6 Presentation skills

This section outlines methods designed to improve your ability to make formal presentations in front of an audience.

Introduction

The ability to make presentations is extremely valuable for the owner manager of a small business. It is useful in pitching for business, putting a case for funding and addressing staff meetings, to name but a few examples. It is also a valuable personal skill to have. It boosts confidence and improves your inter-personal skills. Few people like speaking formally to an audience, but when they realise the benefits and gain experience it often becomes less of a worry and occasionally enjoyable.

Objectives

Before you decide to do a presentation be sure that you have a clear objective. Why are you giving the talk? What do you want your audience to do on the strength of this presentation? When you are planning and performing the presentation keep the objective in mind at all times. This will give your thoughts a focus and will determine the tone of your speech. Having an objective for giving the speech will ensure

that you are not wasting your own and your
audience's time.

Planning the speech

There is no substitute for detailed preparation
and planning. The way you prepare will depend
upon your personal technique and will develop
with experience. Here are some things to
consider:

- Break the task up into manageable units.
  Once you know the length of the
  presentation (eg 15 minutes), break the
  time up into smaller units allocating each to
  different sections of the speech. Then
  tackle each section individually.

- Note down all the points that you want to
  make. Prioritise and order them logically.
  This will help you develop the framework
  and emphasis of the presentation.

- Once you know the basic contents, think
  about the introduction and conclusion of
  the presentation. These are the most
  important parts of the presentation and
  therefore need to have the greatest impact.

- Consider your audience. Their familiarity
  with the subject will determine the level at
  which you pitch the talk. Try to appeal to

what will motivate and interest these people.

- If you can, arrange to visit the venue in advance of the presentation. It helps to be familiar with the environment you are going into. You can also check any facilities you may be planning to use (eg arranging an appropriate layout for the seating).

Structure and content

Keep it short and simple

Too many presentations are simply too long. Few people have the ability to take in every detail of a speech. Usually they remember only two or three key ideas or facts afterwards. Everyone hates long speeches. Do not be tempted to justify yourself by packing the talk with facts and figures. Aim to identify two or three key things that you want to communicate. Concentrate on getting these over in a creative fashion. Also, it is easier to manage and remember a short presentation. If you need to provide more detail, supply a written hand-out.

Structure

A good structure to use is known as 'tell 'em, tell 'em, tell 'em' ie

a) Tell them what you are going to tell them, eg 'In this talk I will endeavour to show …'

b) Tell them. Make the key points expanding and illustrating each one.

c) Tell them what you have told them, eg 'To sum up, I've tried to show …' and conclude.

Introduction

The introduction is the hook that attracts the attention and interest of your audience. It is also critical for your own confidence – if it starts right the rest should follow easily. Your opening words must have impact, they should be short, sharp and to the point. You can attempt to be witty, controversial or even outrageous if the mood of the presentation allows. Whatever you try, attempt to arouse the audience's curiosity. If it helps you to get started you can learn your first few sentences by heart.

Main contents

The main body of the presentation will be dictated by the points that you want to make. Use short, sharp and simple language to keep your audience's attention and to ensure that your message is being understood. Include only one idea per sentence and pause so as to put a mental full-stop between each idea.

Use precise language to convey your message. Your speech should not sound like a reading from a text book, but you do need to convey your message clearly without confusing the salient points with waffle. Try using metaphors and images to illustrate points. This will give what you say impact and help your audience to remember what you have said. But do not try to be too clever.

Concluding

The conclusion should sum up what you have said. The closing seconds of your presentation are as crucial as the opening sentence. Consider what action you would like your audience to take after the presentation is over and attempt to inspire them accordingly.

Visual aids

Visual aids cannot turn a poor speech into a good one, but they can improve upon an already sound presentation. Visuals should only be used as sign posts during the presentation to help the audience understand. Do not cram too much information on to one visual. Include at most six lines and make sure the audience can see the information by using big, bold lettering. Images are usually better than words.

Slide projectors and video machines should be tested out in advance to make sure you know how to operate them. If you intend to use sophisticated technology then have a technician on hand to help out. Practise your speech using the equipment you intend to use. Overheads should be clearly marked and arranged in sequence beforehand. Use a pen to point out details on the overhead projector itself. Do not point to the screen. Flipcharts should be written on quickly in long hand. Try not to turn your back on the audience as you write.

Techniques for speaking

- Try to sound authoritative, sincere and enthusiastic. If you don't have any interest and excitement for your own speech, then don't expect your audience to have any.

- On the day it is very tempting to have a full draft written out in front of you. Don't fall into the trap of simply reading out the text of your speech. Use cue-cards containing headings referring to the main subject areas of your speech and a few crucial details. This will force you to know your speech before the day and encourages spontaneity. String all the cards together in sequence to minimise the chance of losing your place. You may wish to write the introduction out in full on your first card.

- Address your audience directly. Do not look down at the floor. Try to maintain eye contact.

- Your stance, posture and gestures are all important. There are no definite rules. Be aware of how you must be coming across, but try not to be too self-conscious. Don't slouch.

Practice and rehearsal

You don't need to learn your words parrot fashion. What is vital is that you know what you want to say. Have faith in yourself. If you know your subject matter and you have prepared well you will be able to convey your message on the day.

You need to be very familiar with your speech. This can only be achieved through practice. Allow plenty of time to practise before the event. Once you are confident that your presentation is right, resist the temptation to change it. You may have heard the speech many times but the audience will be hearing it for the first time.

If you intend to use any visual aids ensure you have at least one full rehearsal. Make sure you know how to work all the aids. Have a contingency plan to cope with any unforeseen mishaps. If you have any support staff make sure they know what the plan is.

Attitude and stress

Be yourself

There is no one best way to give a presentation. Each person has their own style. Some people prefer to speak off the cuff with no notes. Some people always write the text out and rehearse meticulously. It is important to find a style that suits your own personality. Aim to be natural. Be yourself. If you are trying to be someone that you are not (and get a message across at the same time) the task will be twice as hard.

Be positive

It is all too easy to imagine the whole thing going wrong. This is natural, but do not let it get out of control. Try to cultivate a positive attitude. Review the reasons why you are putting yourself through this and realise it will be worthwhile in the long run. Imagine the whole thing going according to plan. A positive attitude will increase your chances of success on the day.

Stress

You are a bound to get nervous before the performance. Try to view nerves as nervous energy, a force that can be put to positive use. Even experienced actors confess to nerves before performances. Spend a few quiet moments on your own before the presentation to collect your thoughts. Relax your body and breathe deeply, but don't try to fight your feelings of anxiety. Use this time to concentrate on what you are trying to achieve. Make sure that you are clear what your objective is. Above all, have faith in your preparation. Believe that your system will work.

Concentrate on the task

If all else fails, remember that your prime purpose is to communicate a message to the audience. Even if you make a hash of things, if you have said what you had to say you will have succeeded. When you stand up, direct your thoughts to the subject in hand and you will not go far wrong. The audience are there to listen to your speech, not to waste everybody's time by upsetting your presentation.

Vocal delivery

As has been mentioned, aim for a style that suits your own personality. As you gain experience you will pick up some of the finer points of public speaking.

Vocal expression

The voice has many qualities which enhance the message. Volume, pitch, speed of delivery can all be varied to underline your meaning. A common mistake is speaking too fast. Take your time.

Emphasis

Emphasising particular words for effect is an ancient art, and much more difficult than it might appear. The golden rule is to use such dramatic effects sparingly. Do not ham it up!

Articulation

Most people need to articulate their words more clearly when addressing an audience. There is no opportunity for the audience to ask you to repeat a word they might have missed. Aim to sound the vowels and consonants of words clearly. This does not mean talking like an elocutionist. Do not disguise your accent.

A good way to practise the skills of delivery is to read aloud from famous speeches or favourite texts, being conscious at various times of each dimension of vocal delivery. Having said this do not allow your voice to develop unnaturally. When speaking in public you should not be conscious of your delivery.

USEFUL TIPS

● *Avoid too many statistics in your presentations. Include them in a handout that can be distributed to the audience.*

● *Never apologise for giving your presentation. This undermines your self-confidence and the audience's perception of you.*

● *If you forget your words, pause for a moment and remember your objective. The exact words may not come flooding back but at least you will get your message across which is the main thing.*

● *If you need to give the same presentation more than once (ie to different audiences) do not change it once you are happy with it. It may no longer inspire you but it can still be fresh for a new audience.*

● *Go on a public speaking course. This will give you confidence, experience and useful tips for the future.*

7 Stress management

This section discusses stress and introduces the reader to some of the more well known methods for dealing with it.

Introduction

Running a small business is very stressful. Leading a 'normal' family life is difficult. You often need to work late and at weekends. You may not bother to take holidays. Dealing with staff problems can be particularly stressful. If business is not so good, the uncertainty also adds to the stress. It is very important not to get into a vicious circle where anxiety begins to affect your performance, in turn creating more anxiety and so on. Stress can be positive, even stimulating, but if you sense that it is becoming a real problem it is important to recognise the fact and to take some positive action. Find out how to relieve your stress and organise your life in a way that helps you to minimise the problem. If necessary, get professional advice. Look out for signs of stress in your staff and help them to deal with it.

The symptoms of stress

Stress is a physical reaction to a threatening situation. Heart rate, blood pressure and breathing rate increase. You perspire more and your muscles tense up. In the short term, energy levels increase, but in the long term you can become exhausted and underweight. Links between stress and illness are well established. The list includes heart disease, strokes, kidney damage and disturbance of blood sugar levels.

Many people thrive under stress. They are able to use stress reactions to their advantage. Even so, they may still have medical problems in the long term. For most people, stress is extremely debilitating and prevents them from functioning to their full potential. In critical situations you become nervous and embarrassed. Instead of thinking clearly, you become preoccupied with negative thoughts. It is hard to think clearly and to take decisions. Concentration declines and you can become forgetful.

Working with someone showing signs of stress can be irksome. They can become very negative, pessimistic, hypersensitive to criticism and aggressive. It is difficult to enjoy things. Creativity is stifled. Self-esteem can disappear. Over a prolonged period there is the danger of serious depression.

The stress build-up

Some stress is immediate, focused around a particular event or crisis. Stress can also build up gradually, over a long period of time. A variety of factors can contribute to the build up. The stressful events in life are obvious, eg becoming a parent, illness in the family, moving house, starting a new job, divorce, bereavement, dismissal, etc. It is important to understand your various sources of anxiety. Watch out for times when a number of stressful events coincide, and plan accordingly.

Make a list of the things which most cause you anxiety. Try to look at each one in turn. Individually, each worry looks less formidable. Make a realistic assessment of the worry. Why are you worrying about this? Are you being reasonable? Are the consequences you imagine likely to happen? If it is a genuine worry, are you going to do anything about it? If not, why is it bothering you? Most importantly, can you rationalise things? Are you trying to do too much?

Similarly, stress can build up in the course of the day. It is important to understand how you function during the day, eg if you are a morning person, do the stressful things early. Build in breaks throughout the day. It is all too easy keep going when you feel strong. Discipline yourself to stop and relax (see below) regularly, before you feel you need to. If you do this, you will actually achieve more and be less inclined to run out of steam towards the end of the day.

Unrealistic expectations and standards

One of the most common causes of stress is unrealistic expectations about what you can achieve. It is all too easy to overestimate what can be done in the course of one day. If you are setting impractical targets for business success you could be condemning yourself to overwork for the indefinite future. On a more trivial level, if you are a perfectionist, the ordinary untidiness of everyday life can be a constant source of irritation. It is impossible to have everything. If you expect to do everything perfectly, you are putting yourself under unnecessary pressure. It is simply not possible to be perfect. Similarly, if you cannot tolerate the fallibility of others, you will create a lot of unnecessary tension amongst staff. For many, being under stress is an important part of their identity, a way to show that they are an important and dynamic person. It is important to recognise that you have limitations. If you are overdoing it you will in fact be less effective. If you work within your limitations you will be more effective in the long run.

Accepting your stress

Attitudes to work and life cannot be changed overnight. It is important to be realistic and to accept that there is a limit to what can be achieved. This applies to the way you tackle stress too. Do not expect to make it disappear overnight. If you are the sort of person who suffers from stress, you will always suffer from it to some extent. What you can do is take positive action to minimise your stress and the effect it has upon you. Stress is an important part of life. It can often be channelled to your advantage. Many people believe that it is possible to overcome ('unlearn') many of your fear reactions, but this does take time. You will often ask 'why am I putting myself through this?' Remember that it is well worth grappling with your negative feelings. With experience, you will be able to overcome them in many situations.

Planning ahead

Good forward planning is the most effective action you can take to counter stress. Long-term plans should be realistic in terms of what you, and your team are capable of. This also applies to your daily action plans. Tackle unpleasant tasks as soon as possible, before they become a source of worry. Be proactive and imaginative about planning rest and relaxation into your life.

When you must cope with a particularly challenging event, plan your preparation well in advance. Anticipate the problems and above all, have faith in the decisions that you take.

Dealing with people

A common source of stress is anxiety about dealing with people, especially anticipating conflict. Assertiveness training can make you more confident in dealing with people and in facing conflict. You cannot keep all the people happy all of the time. Assess the demands being made upon you. Can they be reduced or adapted to better suit your capacity? Reconcile yourself to the fact that you will fail to deliver on some occasions. Linked to assertiveness is delegation. If you are not confident about asking others to do things for you, you will be overloaded with work.

Relieving the symptoms

Everyone is different. There is no single best way to fight stress. It is important to understand how stress affects you as an individual. Different pressures affect people in different ways.

Talking

It's all too easy to get things out of proportion. Talking to friends or colleagues can help you get things into perspective. Talking helps to release some of the stress and prevents it from being bottled up. It also helps you to think things through and to arrive at a solution. It is not always easy to talk on this level. Do what you can to nurture relationships which allow you to express your worries and to get (and to give) positive support. Small business clubs are a good place to meet others with an understanding of the pressures which you face.

Relaxation

It's easy to tell someone to relax, but actually doing it when you feel stressed is another matter. There are many relaxation techniques. Most procedures include some of the following methods:

a) Stand up, stretch and loosen your muscles.

b) Sit or lie in a comfortable position in a quiet place where you will not be disturbed.

c) Gently try to turn your mind to a peaceful thought, eg a calm sea, or a wood at dawn. Think of a place and time when you felt particularly relaxed and imagine yourself there.

d) It can also help to repeat a peaceful word such as 'relax' inwardly.

e) Become conscious of your breathing and let it become slow, deep and rhythmical.

f) Go through each part of your body in turn (eg left foot, left leg, right foot, etc), tense and relax each muscle group until the whole body is relaxed.

g) Continue to relax, breathing deeply and thinking peaceful thoughts for a brief period.

Such methods work more or less effectively, depending on how stressed you are. It is better do this type of exercise two or three times a day, and not only when you have allowed stress to build up to a high level. To do this properly you may need some coaching from an expert.

Exercise

Stress is essentially a physical reaction to some kind of threat, often termed 'fight or flight'. It is easy to lose sight of how much of our time we spend sitting at a desk. Much of our activity can be 'small muscle', eg talking, writing, typing, etc, and this gives an insufficient outlet for your body's sense of alarm. 'Large muscle activity', eg taking a short walk (if only to the other end of the office) or stretching and basic exercise movement helps to release this extra energy removing some of the adrenaline build up. Recreational exercise outside of work (eg running, squash, swimming, etc) also helps. Exercise and a healthy diet will help you cope with stress.

Stimulation and balance

It is all too easy to think that your business is the be all and end all. If you focus your life entirely around work the fears and anxieties surrounding work become exaggerated. If other things occupy your mind, problems at work can be somewhat diluted. If you are too work focused, you risk losing touch with others on a social level. Socialising and active recreation are vital to recharge your batteries and to discharge stress. Having fun and enjoying things outside of work are very important for relieving stress. Above all, make sure you take a holiday every year.

- *Don't panic! Stress is natural reaction to pressure. Be positive. Stress reactions can be reduced with practice and planning.*

- *Get an outlet for your stress that suits you. Excessive smoking and drinking is not advisable!*

- *If you are having serious problems this will affect your business. Talk to your business counsellor and see your doctor before things get out of hand.*

- *Pay attention to the working environment, especially if you work with computers. If it is uncomfortable this will add to stress.*

- *Read more about stress management. If possible get some training. There are a great many different methods and strategies for dealing with stress, far more than can be covered here. Find an approach which suits you.*

8 Writing reports

Introduction

Reports are used regularly in the business world, to convey an idea, message or analysis effectively and clearly. They may be used, for example, as a tool to address a management problem, to apply for funding or to explain to a customer how to deal with a problem. Reports may be written for customers covering areas such as product development, market reports etc. Reports provide information in a standard format, enabling it to be quickly understood and helping to locate information which is of particular interest. It is important that the approach to reports is consistent, clear and easy to follow. Reports are an important communication tool and are a useful aid when a logical approach to a problem is required.

Reports and their uses

Some reports follow very strict guidelines. Organisations may specify the way a report must be laid out (eg European Community grant applications) and provide their own guidelines to follow. This allows them to compare and select a large number of similar applications. Some formats follow a standard pattern widely recognised by many different organisations eg business plans. Many reports are one-offs, and are structured according to the particular subject at hand. Internal reports are normally used to assess management problems, to consider new product development proposals and market development. External reports cover areas such as funding applications, client problems, consulting reports etc.

The format of reports varies depending upon the purpose. Some are more formal than others, but there are some common features. Information is presented in distinct numbered sections in a logical sequence, with certain sections giving overviews and conclusions. A contents page helps the reader to find sections of interest quickly. Reports are very useful for consultation purposes. Initial copies can be circulated to everyone concerned, giving them the opportunity to contribute or identify errors, before a final version is agreed. Reports provide the reader with material which can be read at their leisure, enabling them to consider any relevant matters. This often results in a more constructive and effective decision making process. Producing a report also helps the problem solving process.

Writing the report

Establish the terms of reference

Before you start it is essential to define the objectives of the task, especially if others are involved. What is the report to cover, what do you expect to get out of it, and what is the submission date? There may be a programme of research for the report. This must be planned out and budgeted for.

Map out the contents

It is often useful to produce some notes on paper which may help to generate ideas for the report. Pattern notes allow you to map out your thoughts and identify key areas. This helps you identify related points which can then be grouped under various headings. Sections should follow on from one another in a logical manner. These notes will frequently take the form of a contents page for the report with numbered sections. If you are producing a one-off report in consultation with others, it is a good idea to circulate your sketch of the proposed contents before you start. This should ensure that the project gets off to the right start.

Think and analyse

The logic and coherence of the report is everything. This is what makes it easy to read and easy to write. Producing a report also helps you to solve problems, so it is important to think things through before you commit them to paper. If you encounter difficulties in writing certain sections, think about the issue again more deeply. If you do not fully understand the subject it is much harder to write about it. Many difficulties in writing and language originate in unclear thinking.

Building up the report

For large reports, each section can be built up separately. It is often useful to start your research by writing out those sections of the report which you already understand and know. This helps you to identify more clearly the gaps in your knowledge which need to be filled. For this reason, access to a word processor makes report production much easier. Some word processing packages also provide built in report formats. You can also plunder sections from previous reports to save on re-writing, and you can switch sections around as your ideas develop. Another way to build up the report is to develop each section on separate sheets which are kept in sequence in a loose-leaf binder. This should reduce the amount of re-writing you need to do.

Presentation

Layout depends upon personal preference. It should be clear and attractive eg wide margins, and clearly defined headings, attractive fonts etc. Pages should look well spaced and easy to read. If you are likely to produce a lot of reports, it may be worth buying a spiral binding machine and having special covers printed with your logo.

Style

In a formal report it is normal to write in the third person ie 'XYZ Pizzas should...' not 'you should...' If you can get away with more informal language do so because it is more readable and you can use simpler language. Adjust the language of the report to suit the reader. Also bear in mind what the reader already knows and not what you presume them to know. Do not use jargon.

Format

There are no set guidelines which are to be used to produce a standard report, but the section headings below should help. It is good practice to number and title each of your sections, and to give subsection numbers too. For example,

3.0 The Market

3.1 Trends

3.2 Customers... etc

Strike a balance. Do not create too many subsections, or subsections of subsections.

Title page

The title page normally gives the author, title, the recipient and the date.

Contents page

The contents page is very important. It gives the reader an overview of the subject at a glance. If you develop the contents page as you write the report, it will help you map out the subject and achieve an overview. The numbered sections of the report are listed in sequence. Some contents pages are very detailed and show every subsection heading too. This helps the reader take in the contents at a glance.

Terms of reference

Terms of reference usually outline the purpose of the report, who it was commissioned by and its submission date. The terms of reference section is sometimes combined with the Introduction, depending on personal preference. If there is any ambiguity in the brief for the report then it is important that it is cleared up before your research actually begins.

Introduction

An introduction to a report will normally give a brief background to the contents of the report, to enable its reader to visualise the situation, if no prior knowledge exists.

The introduction puts the report into context for the reader. It will also often contain the methods of investigation for the report. It is important that a well presented summary is given at the beginning, as the reader may not always read each section of the report, especially if it is quite detailed.

Methodology

If research is involved, many reports, especially market research reports, have a section which describes the way the research was carried out (eg desk research, questionnaire, interviews etc).

Findings

The findings are normally divided between various sections, depending upon the complexity of the case. A different section is normally allocated to each separate area of information. This makes it easier to identify individual areas of concern. The sections should follow a systematic order. It is important that this section is very clearly defined and accurate as it will provide the basis for the remainder of your discussion eg your recommendations.

Conclusions

This section summarises the main points of the report, giving a brief overview of what has been discussed. The recommendations section may sometimes be combined with this.

Recommendations

The recommendations will offer a solution to any problems which have arisen within the main body of findings. The style of writing in this part of the report should be persuasive and positive and should instil confidence in the reader. Recommendations should be realistic and practical. Numerous recommendations should be listed separately so that they can be clearly understood.

Appendix

The appendix usually contains material which may be used as a reference throughout the report eg leaflets, copies of questionnaires and statistical information etc. This section is often invaluable, providing back up material to your findings and recommendations. This section also allows the author to add material without having to re-write the whole report.

Acknowledgements/ references/bibliography

This section includes references which have been used in conjunction with the contents of the report. There is a set format which should be used to cite references, which should be available from your local library. The reference should include the author's name, the publication title, the date, the publisher's name and the page number.

USEFUL TIPS

● *Keep the report brief and concise. Write to express, not to impress. Avoid jargon and ambiguity. Keep all points relevant to the purpose of the report.*

● *Draw up guidelines for staff to follow if you wish to create your own in-house style.*

● *Always be prepared to go back and rethink the fundamental points if you get stuck. Talking it through with colleagues also helps to clarify ideas. When writing, always keep the main purpose of the report in mind.*

● *If you are publishing your report, check the copyright position. You may need permission to use data, or to quote other authors.*

9 Project planning and scheduling methods

This section looks at methods of planning and scheduling that are useful in both manufacturing and service contexts.

Introduction

Most manufacturing operations need to establish specific planning and scheduling systems to ensure that they can deliver their products on time. People often assume that such methods, using charts and such like, are too complicated for non-specialists to use. Systematic planning is in fact useful in more situations than is generally realised. It can produce significant savings in time and money, save stress and crisis management, and above all increase the quality of the product or service for the customer.

Project planning

Project planning is used when there is a definite start and end to an exercise. This approach helps ensure that almost nothing is forgotten because the process itself makes you take everything into account. Planning in this way gets things in the right order and ensures you can set a realistic deadline for the end of the job. It also increases your efficiency by helping you to spot any peaks or troughs when there is either too much or too little to do.

A Project Planning Sheet for the production of a brochure is shown opposite. Lines or words show where an activity is spread over a few days or weeks, and an asterisk* is used when a particular event happens on a particular day – like the delivery of the brochures from the printer (note: the example shown assumes that the designers you appoint will also organise the print production). The way to start is simply to write down a list of all the things that have to be done, put them in a logical order and finally fill in a Project Planning Sheet with estimates of how long each activity will take. To avoid delays, start long lead time activities as early as possible in the order of events.

The plan can then be used to check regularly on what needs to be done when, and whether everything is going according to plan. It is a tool to be used – not a useless exercise. The Project Planning Sheet needs to be brought up to date regularly because plans always change. This way you can control the changes rather than the changes controlling you. This technique is useful in many different areas – from planning a holiday to organising a summer fair.

Project Planning Sheet

WHEN	MONTH	Sept		October				November					Dec
WHAT	Week commencing	21st	28th	5th	12th	19th	28th	2nd	9th	16th	23rd	30th	7th
Identify image/message/numbers/budget		(23) Office meeting											
Specification document			Draft/circulate/finish										
Identify designers				Research/samples									
Get quotes (send specification)					Mail / submission work	Chase							
Shortlist submissions						Circulate/agree shortlist/shortlist interviews							
Award contract								*					
Refine design									Design meetings	Design work			
(Support any photography work)										—	⌐		
(Support any copy production)										—	⌐		
Approve final designs											* Origination		
Approve any cost adjustments											→*		
Check proofs												*	
Production in progress												—	
Delivery													*
Check quality													*
Check invoices/pay													*

Long term scheduling

Many businesses benefit from having a longer term scheduling chart. For example when negotiating a contract a glance at the chart will show if you have the capacity to meet the extra demand. You may need to schedule it for a later time, or contract the work out.

Master scheduling charts are also good communicators: all staff can see forthcoming workloads and make their own suggestions. Note: this can be crucial when arranging holiday cover at the beginning of the year. A well presented chart will also impress your clients.

The best charts for long-term scheduling are dry wipe boards which can be altered from day-to-day as the situation changes. You can buy shapes and stickers to make up your own chart. You can also buy charts for particular types of business. A useful format is to have columns for each month and horizontal sections to group similar activities (eg promotion, client projects, administration etc). Items can be written in or a symbolic system (see illustration) can be used.

Every business works to different time horizons. Normally long- term schedules are reviewed on a monthly basis, when more detailed plans for the month are drawn up. This is the time to look at what will be coming up over the long term – it's surprising how often you will have forgotten something obvious (eg getting your year end accounts sorted out could interfere with work you had planned to do for a customer). If all the team are involved in this, you are more likely to spot future bottle-necks.

When new commitments are taken on, it is crucial that they are marked into the schedule immediately – especially if a number of people use the chart.

Event schedules

It is sometimes necessary to put together a meticulous plan for a specific day. Very few businesses can operate without having to organise some kind of an event. It may be to launch a new product, it may be a press call, it may be part of a package of work you are doing for a client. Whatever it is, it is crucial that everything runs smoothly if your customers are to believe that you are a professional outfit. On such occasions your company is on show.

Planning for the event should be done as a project plan, and the workloads programmed into the long-term schedule. In addition a master schedule for the event can be very useful. The schedule (running to no more than two pages) should summarise everything about the occasion. It should contain:

- An outline with specific times of everything that must be done during the day, and who will do it, from the first arrival to packing up and finishing.

- Key events/moments (eg 'arrival of guests', 'presentation starts', etc) incorporated into the schedule with times.

- A list of everyone involved, including those you might have contracted in support, listing their responsibilities for the day.

- Contact information (eg organiser, venue manager, etc), and any other important facts or instructions you want to stress.

- It is often helpful to attach a map of the venue to the schedule.

Make up the schedule when you first plan out what will happen and update it as things develop, providing all those involved with a revised copy. Making up a master schedule is an excellent prompt to force you to think of everything, and is a useful document for future reference. Paper is kept to a minimum and you can be confident that everyone has been put in the picture and knows what they have to do. This is particularly useful if sub-contractors (eg caterers, stage managers, etc) do not live up to expectations. On the day of the event, the schedule serves as a handout for a team briefing session before the action starts.

- *There is now a wide range of software, eg Microsoft Project available to assist the planning process. These packages can produce charts, schedules, etc very rapidly.*

- *'Keep it simple' is a golden rule of planning – if you don't understand your own system you are in trouble. Apply the ideas in this section only in so far as they are useful for your own situation. Periodically review the methods you use to plan; they may no longer be appropriate.*

- *There are a number of computerised systems available that allow you to produce planning charts ranging from personal diaries to larger specialised production systems. A small business should be cautious about adopting such packages which can be expensive. Make sure your hardware, software, and your own computer skills are fully up to speed before relying on such systems for planning.*

10 Problem solving and business decisions

This section looks at problem solving methods with particular reference to business decisions.

Introduction

Problem solving and decision making methods are closely related. The need to solve specific problems occurs throughout the business operation. Decision making may be described as problem solving in the particular area of business strategy. Both involve a logical and systematic approach to define and analyse the problem, generate possible solutions and to identify the best option.

Running a business is all about taking decisions. It is very tempting to take snap, 'instinctive' decisions. This is often necessary and sometimes very effective. All the same, such decisions can too often be the easiest, short-term option, which does not address the underlying problem. You may not have taken into account all the information available. Worse still, there may be others with more relevant knowledge which you can use, or who have already thought of an ingenious solution. However good you may feel your instincts are, there is also a place for a more rational process to help you to identify solutions. Most problem solving methods are quite straightforward and involve nothing more sophisticated than paper, pencil and a little time for thought and discussion. Do not bang your head off a brick wall; use your intelligence to solve your problems.

Barriers

The first step in finding a solution is to recognise that a problem exists. The reaction to problems can often be to ignore them, to work harder (rather than smarter) or to find someone to blame. If you feel under pressure, tackling the problem itself can seem like the worst option. It is tempting to put it off for another time. Solving problems requires an investment of time. You may not feel that you have the time available. The problem may seem formidable. You may doubt your ability to come up with a solution. You may fear losing face if you get it wrong.

Do not prevaricate. If you have a serious problem, the sooner you face up to it the better. If you have lots of problems, prioritise and tackle the most important ones first. Set aside time on a regular basis to think through your problems – this is a very important management function. Make sure you will not be disturbed. Use a systematic approach. The problem solving process is designed to break things down and make them seem less formidable. Do not be afraid to ask your own staff for help, or to seek help from an external adviser.

The problem solving process

There is a well tried, logical framework for thinking through problems and coming up with solutions. The process is similar to the framework used in strategic documents such as business plans and reports. Whilst this might seem too involved for everyday use, the same basic approach can be applied to any problem, using paper and pencil. Often, a suitable solution will come up quite quickly, once you start thinking it through. If you are working alone use pencil and paper. If you are working in a group, use a flip chart.

Define the problem

What exactly is the problem? Pin it down exactly. The problem may not be what you first thought it was. Sometimes a solution can present itself at this early stage. How extensive, how important is the problem? Do you just need half an hour to think it through by yourself, or, do you need to call a meeting? Do you need to commission some research? If the decision affects others, do you need to seek their views before you put forward a solution?

Search for relevant information

Sketch out what you already know about the problem. Talk to your colleagues, and check your files to fill in the gaps. Do not forget to consult your own planning notes. You may have thought this through before. Do you have an ideas file, or a suggestions file to call on? Refer to your business plan; it should provide the strategic framework for most of your operational decisions. On a less formal level, talk to one or two colleagues and bounce ideas around. Is there a basic book or manual which might contain a straightforward solution to your problem?

Analysing information

Analysis is the process of breaking things down and giving them a structure that you can understand. It can often be quite a playful process where you put things in order and look for patterns. It helps you understand the problem better and should make it seem far less formidable. A very simple method is to list pros and cons for each option. It can be helpful to break down the information under headings. Any documentation you create may be useful for future reference. The journalist's six questions can be useful – what, why, when, how, where and who? Mapping out problems as flow charts or pattern notes is also useful. Again, discussion is very useful for working through ideas. Can you identify the critical areas which need the most thought and attention, which form the 'heart' of the problem?

Generate a range of options

Do not be tempted to go for the first idea that comes into your head. Set up a number of scenarios and look at the consequences of each. This is the stage where you need creative thinking. Use a brainstorming session (see over). Use the opportunity to involve others in coming up with solutions, especially the creative and imaginative people in your team. Try not to create false expectations that all their suggestions will be used.

Evaluate options and decide

Review your objectives. Look at each option critically. Which best meets your objectives? Can you balance this against the risks in each case? What are the cost implications? When you have weighed up the options, it is absolutely essential that you go on and take a decision. It is only worth setting aside time to solve problems if you are also prepared to set a time limit and commit yourself to a decision at the end of the process. Do not get stuck in 'paralysis by analysis'. You may not be entirely comfortable with your solution, but you have given it thought and now you must make a commitment. If it is a group decision, or a solution suggested by one person, give the decision your full backing. Do not discourage participation by blaming others if the solution does not work.

Quick decisions

Decisiveness is an essential leadership quality. Work teams look to their leader to take responsibility and act on their judgement. Decisions, if they are not to be random, need to be based upon a frame of reference. In order to decide, you have to know what it is you want from your business. If you do not have strong feelings about what you are doing, it will be difficult to take decisions about it. At the businesses level, a wider strategic awareness of your objectives and strategies provides you with the framework for your day-to-day decisions. If this is not clear, it will be hard to decide.

Even so, there are still many occasions when you do have to take snap decisions. This is all about confidence. On the whole, it is better to act than not to act. You can only judge your decisions by their results. You can only learn more about your business and what you want from it by taking decisions. The only way to improve your judgement is by constantly testing it out. Do not be tempted to act impulsively. If you are under stress or angry, you may do something stupid. Try to settle yourself and calm down before you start to think about solutions.

Brainstorming

Brainstorming is a well tried method of generating ideas. It is a relaxed approach which aims to get you to search out all the ideas lurking in the back of your mind. Brainstorming is normally done in a group. The aim is to create an atmosphere and momentum that throws up more and more ideas. You normally require a quiet room and a flip chart or white board to write down the suggestions. The session may be called to generate solutions, or the group may be involved in the whole problem solving process. However you approach it, it is important that the problem is well defined for the group before the session starts.

The group is then encouraged to come up with ideas. Everyone should realise that at this stage any idea, no matter how far fetched, is acceptable. It is a rule that no-one is allowed to criticise or mock unusual ideas. In fact 'way out' ideas should be encouraged (the person writing down the ideas should write down exactly what was suggested). This should create a relaxed 'fun' atmosphere where people are searching in their minds for anything they can think of to solve the problem. Sometimes the idea that at first seemed impossible is the best option. Usually the atmosphere of open minded discussion throws up an obvious solution which for some reason had been overlooked. It is important to set a time limit. Brainstorming should be followed by a critical analysis by the group of each idea. The best solutions should be identified and acted upon.

Problem solving in teams

Problem solving requires a combination of a logical and creative thinking. To an extent these are contradictory qualities, which is why it can be helpful to involve a number of people in the process. You may have a particular member of staff who is particularly good at problem solving. Use this person whenever you can. It is important to encourage an open-minded and trusting environment where everyone feels able to identify problems and suggest solutions. Using groups or teams to solve problems is certainly good practice and produces all sorts of fringe benefits. On the other hand, groups must be managed properly if they are to work effectively. Someone must be responsible for chairing the group, documenting results and commissioning research. Do not appoint a team if the problem does not warrant it or if the results are unlikely to be used.

- *After analysing a problem, it can help to allow time for your subconscious to work on a solution. Sleep on it.*

- *Taking decisions is the essence of management. Once you have given the matter due consideration, take the decision and stick to it. You will often feel uncomfortable and doubt that you have done the right thing. You will be criticised, and there will be times when you get it wrong. As a manager it is essential for you to accept the responsibility to trust your judgement and to take critical strategic decisions.*

- *Think about your own particular style of problem solving. What are the barriers which stop you addressing problems? What are your strengths and weaknesses when it comes to solving problems.*

Working with teams

part
three

11 Delegation

This section looks at ways to encourage your team to support you more effectively.

Introduction

Delegation is not just about giving tasks to others. It is about getting the people who work for you to take full responsibility for certain key functions. In order for a business to grow (and for employees to find new paths of development), new people must be employed to take over established functions allowing others to develop new aspects of the business. Owner managers tend to like being in control of everything. They find it difficult to let go of things which they have created and nurtured, yet this is exactly what they must do if the operation is to grow and develop. Delegation is also an important dimension of the Total Quality Management approach where all staff take responsibility for quality and are involved in the operational decisions which affect them.

Obstacles to delegation

Why do people find it difficult to delegate?

- Time. It seems quicker to do it yourself than to bother explaining the task and correcting mistakes.

- Doubt. Choice brings the fear that the person will not be successful, and will leave even more problems than they solve.

- Status. An employee who is quick on the uptake and does well can take over the role of being the person everyone goes to with their problems. You may feel threatened by their competence. They may even find something wrong with the way you do things.

- Confidence. If you find it hard to give instructions, this will be an obstacle. You will put off delegating. If problems arise, or if the person fails to discharge their responsibilities, you may doubt your own ability to confront the person about their actions.

- Staff development. Having given your staff increased responsibilities, you may not be confident of being able to reward them sufficiently. Conversely, some people hesitate to delegate tasks which are too tedious.

- Method. You know you need to delegate, but you do not know where to start.

Benefits of delegation

To counter the negative aspects of delegation, review the benefits:

- Personal effectiveness. Delegating tasks allows you to concentrate on the things you do best, and will allow you to tackle more interesting and challenging things in the future. Decisions are less likely to be put off.

- Growth. Passing tasks down the line is essential if you want the business to grow. Not knowing how to do this is recognised as one of the biggest obstacles to small business growth. More time should be available to think strategically about business growth.

- Staff development. If staff are not to get bored they need new challenges. Delegation helps you test out their ability to increase their contribution to the business. Staff can take quick decisions themselves, and will have a better understanding of the details concerned. Good delegation should improve the overall productivity of your employees.

- Management. Dealing with staff may seem a difficult problem, but that is what management is all about. It is too easy to withdraw into 'essential' tasks and not develop relations with your staff. The bottom line is that it is wasteful for senior staff to be paid for doing low value work.

Delegation is not an easy option. It does not make things easier (there will always be other challenges), but it does make things more efficient and effective. It is essentially a more interactive way of working with the team of people around you – involving instruction, training and development. You must invest time and effort to do it effectively.

When to delegate

Delegation is fundamental to management. Look for opportunities to do it. Delegate when you find that you simply have too much work to do. Delegate when you cannot spend enough time on the things you know are important. Delegate when you realise that you need to develop your staff (this is especially important when a new employee starts with you). Finally, delegate when you know that a particular member of staff has the special skills which suit them for a task.

What to delegate

* Delegate routine administrative tasks which take up too much of your own time. There may be small routine things which you have always done, which you even enjoy doing

(eg sending your own faxes) but are an inappropriate use of your time. Be prepared to look afresh at the little things about work which perhaps you have taken for granted.

• Delegate projects which it makes sense for one person to handle, and will be a good test of how a person manages and co-ordinates. Give the person something they can do. Don't hand out impossible tasks which others have failed at. This will be a bad experience for the person concerned.

• Delegate tasks for which the person has a special aptitude.

• Delegate liaison with a particular person or organisation which is important, but can be time consuming.

To whom to delegate

Staff development is a vital part of delegation. It is essential to have a good understanding of the people you delegate to. Adapt your approach according to the individual. They must have the skills and ability or at least the potential to develop into the role. They must be someone you can trust. Find out who can do what by testing them out with small tasks. Do they show good time management skills? Do they keep a diary? Do they make notes? You may decide to give training, or develop these skills in the person through delegation. Make sure that the employee is available for the assignment, don't overburden the people who do effective work. Try to spread your delegations among as many employees as possible. Don't overlook the possibility of assigning a task to two or more people.

How to delegate

- Attitude. Think positive. You have the right to delegate. You must delegate. It is worth doing. You will not do it perfectly first time. Your ability to delegate will improve with experience. Do not prevaricate. Take decisive action. If need be, learn more about the skills of assertiveness. A positive approach will also give the person to whom you delegate confidence in themselves. Make them feel that you believe in them.

- Plan. If you expect the person to be efficient, it is important to be organised yourself. If you do not have an overall plan of what is going on, it will be hard to identify, schedule and evaluate the work you ask others to do. Schedule the necessary time to develop the person in the job. Assess the person. Do you have a plan for their development? Do you have notes about how they are doing?

Assess the task. Decide how much responsibility you are prepared to give the person. Prepare before you see the person, but do not make this a pretext for delay.

- Discussion. Discuss the tasks and the problems in depth. Explain fully what you expect them to do. It is crucial to give the person precise objectives, but you may choose to encourage the person to seek these out themselves by letting them ask you questions. Ask questions and get suggestions. Let them participate in setting the parameters. Ensure they understand why they are doing the task, where it fits into the scheme of things. Ask them how they will go about the task, discuss the plan and the support they might need.

- Targets. Set deadlines and schedule them into your diaries. Summarise what you have agreed and take notes about what you want them to do. If you are giving the person a lot of creative scope and testing them out, you may decide to be deliberately vague. If the task is urgent and critical, you must be very specific.

- Support. The degree of support you give will depend upon the development of the person, and your relationship with them. In the early stages it can be appropriate to work with the person, to share certain tasks. You will be able to back off more as your understanding of the person's abilities increases. Encourage them to come back to you if they have any problems. Whilst it is important to have time to yourself, make yourself accessible should the person have a problem, or the situation change. If they need you to check something over, try to get it back to them quickly. Do not interfere or criticise if things are going according to plan.

- Monitor progress. It is too easy to forget all about the task until the completion date. In the meantime all sorts of things could have gone wrong. When planning, build in times to review progress. If you expected more problems to arise and have heard nothing, seek the person out. Otherwise schedule routine meetings with the person. Be prepared to alter deadlines and objectives as the situation changes.

- Review performance. Do not promise rewards you cannot deliver. If you increase a person's responsibilities, they should receive fair rewards for it. On the other hand, there may be limits on what you can offer. Rewards might depend upon the overall success of the business. Development can carry its own rewards.

Discuss such career development issues with the employee in appraisals, and ensure you note the results of delegated tasks for this purpose. When a task is complete, give praise and review how it went. If the person has failed to deliver, discuss this too. If you delegate responsibility, it is important to hold people responsible for what they do.

USEFUL TIPS

- *Focus on results rather than methods. To quote Robert Heller, 'If you can't do something yourself, find someone who can and let them do it in their own sweet way'.*

- *Be patient and have faith in the people around you.*

- *Do not delegate responsibilities without also conferring the authority to discharge those responsibilities.*

12 Managing meetings

This section examines ways to get the most out of the meetings which you are involved with.

Introduction

Formal meetings are an important part of business life. Properly run, a meeting helps a group to agree action with a particular purpose in mind and ensures decisions are recorded and implemented. A number of conventions have grown up around meetings. At best they allow everyone to contribute effectively. At worst proceedings can be stilted and boring. In crucial external meetings it can be very important to know the conventions and how to make an effective contribution. In internal meetings, proceedings should be as efficient and effective as possible in order to get results and not waste people's time. The most effective meetings are those which are well planned, well chaired and where members are relevant and co-operative.

Types of meeting

A meeting is a gathering of people at an agreed time and place with the intention of discussing and agreeing actions and/or policies. Proceedings are governed by rules of conduct which should ensure that matters are properly considered and that all members can contribute. Accountability is a very important feature. Conclusions and action points are recorded, and the results are reviewed at subsequent meetings.

Meetings can be held for a variety of reasons. Some meetings eg board meetings are a legal requirement. Management meetings may be held on a regular basis to monitor the progress of a business, a project or a department. Such meetings tend to be more formal. Decisions are being made and people are reporting back on their actions, so good record keeping and direction are important. Other meetings may be less structured eg regular staff meetings to give information and to air problems or ideas. One-off meetings may be formed to address particular problems. This may be to sort out some dispute or operational problem or a more formalised team meeting eg a special group to look at improving quality in a particular area.

This section concentrates mainly on the more formal type of meeting where continuing accountability and positive direction are of particular importance. Nevertheless if you are serious about getting results, even from relatively informal meetings, applying some basic rules of conduct and minuting is advised.

When to use meetings

It is important to know when a meeting is appropriate and when it is not. Use meetings only if they are necessary and justified. Ask yourself if a meeting is really necessary. Do not use meetings if you want speedy action. Reconciling conflicting opinions and ideas is usually time consuming. Is the end result likely to be over-ruled? Do you really require a range of opinion or is the question best addressed by one person?

Purpose

First and foremost, any meeting should have a specific purpose in mind. Too many meetings are routine talking shops held to flatter or to make people feel they are involved. Clearly this is a waste of time. If the real decisions are taken elsewhere, the meeting will usually be counter-productive. Any meeting formed should have a declared and specific purpose in mind, and should have the full backing of senior management. The purpose will usually be encompassed in a title which heads agendas and minutes.

Co-ordination and involvement

Meetings are useful when you need to draw on the expertise (and sometimes the authority) of a number of people, in order that balanced and informed decisions can be made. They also ensure that everyone involved has had an input, or at the very least, they are aware of what has been decided. Subsequent action should be more co-ordinated as a result, and the level of commitment should be much higher.

Considering issues

Meetings are also valuable if a lot of care and consideration is required in addressing a problem. They can encourage members to consider the reasoning behind proposals more carefully. Additional expertise can be introduced from other organisations as needed, and investigations can be commissioned and evaluated.

Teamwork

At the very basic level, regular meetings are a good way to keep in touch with what is going on in the business and to foster team spirit. Regular meetings force everybody to talk to each other and to address problems which could otherwise get out of hand.

Basic rules

Like a court of law, meetings should follow a 'due process' if decisions are to be seen as reasonable and fair. The rules may be more or less apparent depending upon the level of trust and compatibility of the group members.

- Members must attend on time, pay attention and take an active part in proceedings.

- An agenda should be agreed and followed.

- Members should prepare for meetings in advance and should act on the instructions of the group.

- Members must accept the authority of the chair to organise proceedings.

- Everyone must have the opportunity to make themselves heard.

- A record should be taken of decisions reached and it should be ratified by the group before circulation.

It helps to follow similar rules in your more informal team meetings. Give everyone a chance to contribute. Make it clear when it is time to take a decision. Summarise and pin down decisions and make a record of what has been agreed – even if this is just your own written record.

The chair

The 'chairperson' or 'chair' is the guardian of the rules. Without an effective chair, meetings tend to be dominated by the most forceful individual and the results are distorted.

The person

The chair will often limit their own contribution to summarising and directing proceedings and giving a casting vote. In reality, the chair will also contribute their own thoughts, especially in management meetings. If you are chairing such meetings it is important to balance your contribution. If you really just want to hand out instructions, do not bother with a formal meeting.

The authority of the chair must be unquestioned. This authority need not be formal. Successful chairs are usually of a character which lends itself to the task. They need to be calm, even handed and clear thinking. Above all, they need to be good listeners. Experience in handling meetings is obviously an asset. A sense of humour also helps. They should be assertive enough to deal with any challenge to their authority.

Directing proceedings

The chair normally opens the meeting with a short speech, detailing the main purpose of the meeting and welcoming members present.

They should check that the minutes have been read and that all members agree with them. The agenda is often previewed at the outset, and times allocated to items. The group may decide to make certain alterations. Additional matters may be discussed under any other business. The chair should ensure that the agenda is followed, stays on schedule, and that discussion does not stray off the point in question.

Stimulating discussion

The chair may stimulate discussion by asking questions. This is especially useful for encouraging the more reticent members to contribute. The chair should ensure everyone contributes and should prevent one person from dominating. It is very helpful for the chair to summarise the main points at regular intervals. This gives a sense of progress and keeps discussion on the right track.

Reaching decisions

It is particularly important to clarify when a decision needs to be made, what that decision is and who is responsible for taking action. This is where the art of chairing is critical. The chair needs to be able to sense when a consensus is or is not being reached. In other situations, the chair may need to take a unilateral decision if the group cannot agree. Voting should generally be avoided except in very formal meetings. At the close the chair should suggest an appropriate time and date for the next meeting and thank everyone for attending.

The agenda

The agenda is a list of the items to be covered in the meeting. It can also act as the notification to members that the meeting is to take place. The document will include the title of the meeting, the place and time and the members of the group. Ideally the agenda should be prepared by (or at least discussed with) the chair, before circulation. The agenda ought to be circulated to members in advance, along with the minutes from previous meetings, allowing enough time to read them before the next meeting.

Place routine matters early in the agenda eg apologies, matters arising etc. Brief or urgent matters should also be covered early, followed by any business arising from the last meeting. New items should be considered next and arranged in a logical sequence. Give a brief overview of points raised in the previous meeting. List topics to be discussed in priority order. Distinguish items for discussion and items requiring decisions. Plan the amount of time to be spent on each item, considering the number of people attending the meeting and the complexity of the issues.

Minutes

Minutes may be recorded by the chair or a designated group member. If uncertain about which points should be recorded, the designated person should consult the chair. If one member feels strongly that a certain point should be recorded, this should be done. In any event, the chair will normally review the notes and delete any unnecessary items. It is an important principle that decisions, recommendations and responsibilities are recorded, and that all members have the opportunity to approve this record. Recording the substance of discussions is less important. The best minutes are in the form of a list (sometimes numbered) of recommendations with the initials of those responsible for action next to them. In addition to the title of the working group and the date and time of the meeting, list the group members that were present at the meeting, and record apologies for absentees.

- *Prepare for meetings well in advance.*

- *It is useful to understand something about how people behave when they are in a group. See 'Approaches to team building' (section one).*

- *It is vital to listen. This helps to ensure that your own points are relevant and are listened to. It is important to make your points as brief and concise as possible. Be persuasive but never pushy. You will be more successful if your points are well presented and give your colleagues something to think about.*

- *Do not pad out meetings to fit the time available. If there is general agreement and you get ahead of schedule, finish early.*

13 Motivating staff

This section looks at various ways leaders can motivate the people who work for them.

Introduction

The ability to motivate is a key skill of leadership, and essential for anyone employing a team of people. Some people have a natural aptitude for motivating a team. Others find it more difficult. By understanding more about what motivates people, and learning a few simple methods, your ability to motivate others can improve. With experience, you will further develop your own particular approach to motivating others to perform at work. Much has been written on the subject and many different theories exist. This section concentrates on practical methods rather than the more involved psychology of motivation.

The importance of motivation

Motivation is a key factor in the effectiveness of individuals at work. A person with great ability is useless if they are not motivated to overcome the problems they face. Poor motivation leads to poor performance. In the worst cases, individuals may become depressed or disruptive. They will certainly bring down the morale of the rest of the team. Motivated employees will make the best of their abilities and be more creative. The bottom line is that motivated employees use their time at work much more productively and therefore deliver better value for money when they are at work. Whilst money is important most people are motivated by other factors. Many employers rely upon fear to motivate staff. Apart from being very destructive in itself this does not encourage loyalty or real effectiveness at work. Maslow showed that when the basic necessities of life have been seen to, the individual becomes concerned with their social position and expressing themselves as an individual.

Leadership

If you wish to motivate others, it is important to be motivated yourself. If you are running your own business and you find it difficult to motivate yourself then clearly this has fundamental implications for the business. On the other hand you can be perfectly confident about the business, yet uncomfortable about how you show this to others. The important thing is to realise that your own behaviour will have an important influence on the people that work for you.

Achievement

Achieving targets boosts self-esteem and motivates people to work towards new targets. Failure to achieve can have the opposite effect. If the direction of the business is unclear or you are vague about what you expect from others, it will be difficult for employees to measure their own success. Targets must be achievable, so that tasks are continually motivating. People need to know what you expect from them, and when they have succeeded in meeting your expectations.

Training

Training is one way to help staff feel more confident about meeting their targets. Going on a course can also be a refreshing change from the everyday routine of work. Courses can also be a form of recognition for the person concerned. Employees also feel encouraged that they are improving their prospects by building up their knowledge and skills. Conversely, if employees are given training of little value, and they must return to a backlog of work as a consequence, this will demotivate. Ensure that when you organise staff training you use the opportunity to motivate.

Stimulation

Routine and repetitive work is boring. Concentration goes down, and mistakes start to occur. Find ways to vary the methods, sequence and pace of work. Specialisation may seem efficient but if the work is boring, motivation will be a problem. Many employers have now moved away from the traditional division of labour where people concentrate on one aspect of the production process. Instead employees work in groups to bring the product right through the production process, from beginning to end. This not only provides variety, it also involves and increases the sense of responsibility and control – all important motivators.

As the famous Hawthorne experiments showed, a simple change in the working environment can lead to increased productivity. You may decide to move the furniture round in the office. Consider the benefit to individuals of working in different departments or out of the office for a while. It may be necessary to have some kind of job rotation system.

Recognition

Most people like to be appreciated. There is nothing worse than labouring away in obscurity without acknowledgement. Money is some compensation, but it is also important to know that others realise what has been achieved. Respect from others is a basic human need. Showing people that they are appreciated can give a tremendous ego boost, and encourages further effort. You should only recognise genuine achievement, so it is important to keep yourself aware of the contribution each individual is making.

A simple 'thank you' is often underestimated. Even if the target is not reached, thank people for their efforts. Routine praise is not effective. Recognition should be done in a natural way. You must genuinely mean it when you give praise. Public recognition (eg award presentations or newsletter profiles) is even more effective.

Responsibility

Individuals can be encouraged to work to their best ability if they are in charge of their own lives and responsibilities. People like to feel that they are in control. Jobs may be made more stimulating by making your staff more accountable and involved. If you interfere frequently, staff can lose their sense of involvement and motivation will suffer.

Career development

Failure to achieve an expected promotion will demotivate. In appraisals ensure the expectations which you both have are realistic. If the possibilities for promotion are limited, ensure that the person is aware of this. You may need to find alternative ways to motivate an ambitious person. Show them how success in the job will lead to opportunities with other employers in due course. Wherever possible, offer opportunities to existing staff rather than recruiting new managers. This should encourage everyone to believe that there are at least some opportunities to develop a career within the business.

Individuals

Take an interest

Do not assume that everyone is motivated by the same thing. Knowing employees individually will help you to establish what the person may be motivated by and their particular needs. Use appraisal records and CVs to help you think about the needs of individuals, but also try to take a genuine interest in the person (inside and outside of work). A person may have personal problems that affect motivation during work. It is all too easy to become obsessed only with tasks and performance. Try to schedule routine contact (eg weekly) to ensure you stay in touch.

Horses for courses

If a person is doing work they are not suited for it is discouraging. Satisfaction comes from doing things you are good at. It is essential to match people with the work they can do. Use training to close any skills gaps. Different jobs require different motivators. Salespeople must be highly motivated. They will be immediately aware of their successes and failures. Their motivations tend to be based upon the pleasure principle.

Problem people

Deal decisively with individuals who are basically not motivated to do the job. You may be wasting time trying to motivate such a person when your time may be better spent supporting more willing people. A disaffected worker will demotivate others.

Motivating the team

Information

Try to keep staff informed about what is going on in the business. If important changes take place out of the blue (eg the arrival of a new employee, the acquisition of new premises etc) employees can feel overlooked and even threatened. Staff meetings, newsletters and circulars should be used to keep everyone aware of what is happening in the business.

Participation

Involving employees in planning and innovation is recognised as a highly effective way to motivate. Apart from the fact that employees can provide a realistic insight into the operation, involvement in management decisions recognises the value of individuals, and is a particularly good way to keep everyone informed about the strategic position of the business.

Meetings

Any meeting you hold should be regarded as an opportunity to motivate. Regular team meetings provide an opportunity for individuals to co-ordinate their efforts and to share problems and solutions. Staff realise their problems are not unique and feel more supported. The leader must make sure the meeting is a positive experience. Problems that come up must be addressed, not brushed aside. Individuals with problems should be reassured and encouraged. Above all, the leader should engender a feeling of confidence and optimism and finish on an upbeat note. There is nothing worse for staff than a reproachful meeting where they all go away feeling that they have 'let down' their leader.

MOTIVATING STAFF

Social activities

Social events allow staff to become more familiar with each other, exchange ideas and develop more of a team spirit. Social events are a good way to give employees a sense of involvement and of being allowed to share in some of the 'perks' of the enterprise. Events can also break down barriers between departments and between managers and staff. Working together on sporting and charity events can also develop team spirit.

USEFUL TIPS

- *There is no one best way to motivate. Try out different methods. Use methods which suit you, your staff and your line of business.*

- *Use humour and your imagination to think of things which will motivate your staff.*

- *The 'One Minute Manager' provides a useful, if simplistic approach ie one minute goal setting, one minute praising and one minute criticism.*

- *Obtain training in the skills of managing people. Contact your local Training and Enterprise Council (Local Enterprise Company in Scotland) for details of courses available.*

14 Mentoring staff

This section describes mentoring and its use within staff development.

Introduction

Mentoring can mean different things to different people. At work, mentoring is usually where one person makes it easier for another to make progress in their learning or personal development. The mentor offers assistance, guidance, advice and support within a relationship which has been arranged for that purpose.

Mentoring has several benefits. Learners are: supported throughout the learning process; helped to understand the organisation better; encouraged to develop their skills and to be aware of their strengths and weaknesses. The process also helps mentors to develop their own skills and job function. In addition, the organisation gains better trained and empowered staff, more effective management development and an orientation towards learning.

What mentors do

Mentors help learners with their integration into a new organisation or work role. They give direction in how things are done within the new job and how the learner might use their own strengths. Mentors focus on the development of their learner, giving time and attention to an extent that few managers could. Development occurs 'as required', paced to suit the learner.

Mentors have to take on various roles

Mentor as coach

Coaching can help in developing a learner's ability to co-operate and collaborate. It works best when the mentor is supportive and offers friendly encouragement. Mentors must be careful when providing coaching or feedback that has not been sought. It is important not to intrude upon someone else's (eg a line manager's) area of responsibility; it is also important not to damage the relationship with the learner. Mentors should not be responsible for their learner's work performance.

Mentor as counsellor

Counselling skills enable mentors to help learners cope with any difficulties and take advantage of the learning opportunities open to them. Mentors use counselling techniques to empower their learners, building their confidence and reducing their uncertainties.

Mentor as role model

Mentors, by their behaviour, should demonstrate the acceptable standard of conduct. From this, learners should be able to judge how they might fit within the organisation.

Mentoring in practice

Mentoring has various characteristics. It is extremely flexible with regard to how and where it is used. It can be informal, occurring away from normal work. It can be highly work focused and practical. It can be tailored to fit the needs and interests of the individual. It takes into account values, motives and emotions. It includes a feedback system, which can engage interest and enhance learning. Mentoring can encompass a whole range of activities and can operate alongside other learning methods.

During the first meeting with a learner, a mentor should spend most of the time finding out about them in an unthreatening way. It is important for the learner to trust the mentor and feel that they have their best interests at heart. Mentoring works best if the learner can speak freely about their concerns, knowing that what they say will be kept confidential.

Approaches to mentoring

The skills, qualities and attributes needed by mentors vary with the aims and objectives of the mentoring process and the approach taken to meet them. There are several approaches to mentoring. You can use one, or a combination of, the following:

Informal

Informal mentoring occurs all of the time, whether planned or not. It occurs when someone finds a more experienced employee or manager whom they respect and feel they can readily relate to and confide in.

Role model

It is inevitable that a mentor will be a role model for those they are developing. The learner will be influenced by the mentor's attitudes, values, problem solving techniques and treatment of other people.

The 'sponsor' system

Under the sponsor system, the mentor provides a wide variety of experience for the learner through special projects and assignments. In these cases, the mentor would usually be a senior manager, with maturity, influence and credibility. The mentor would introduce the learner to key people in the organisation and ensure that suitable projects and tasks were set, to allow a learner's achievements to be widely recognised. This system is particularly useful for developing an individual or group of people in order to meet known short-term needs.

Peer group mentoring

There are various approaches to this type of mentoring. For learners who are new to the organisation, the system can be used to provide them with a friend who is responsible and able to pass on good advice. The young people appointed as mentors gain an introduction to management skills. When appointing these mentors, you should look towards people with 2-3 years experience and a positive attitude towards their work. Peer group mentoring can be particularly useful for small firms, letting them make greater use of their resources by selecting, training and using existing staff to develop others.

Self-development mentoring

This approach encourages learners to take responsibility for themselves and to make use of any development opportunities which the employer may provide. Independence and self-determination are promoted in the individual learners. As a group, learners are expected to identify the strengths and resources they have between them, and to use these by keeping in regular contact with one another.

Managers as mentors

Managers becoming involved in the development of learners can find that their job is enriched and they themselves feel more motivated. They should have a track record of developing staff, maturity, good judgement and the necessary time to spend in the job. It is important that they are competent in giving feedback, coaching, counselling and other inter-personal skills.

Counselling

What is counselling?

Counselling is a way of helping people to make their own decisions and to help themselves. Its main aims include helping someone to see their present situation more clearly, understand fully their feelings about it, determine what action, if any, they want to take, and make realistic plans for achieving the desired result.

When to counsel

Situations arise where counselling may be necessary. They typically tend to involve problems, frustrations and/or relationship difficulties. The situation may well be having a negative impact on the individual. There are often also unknown factors, such as why things are occurring the way they are, and what should be done about it. The individual being counselled will be involved at a personal level, bringing emotions and values into consideration.

Steps in the counselling process

Establish the relationship

The learner must have trust in the counsellor and must feel that they are easy to communicate with. It is also important that the learner feels that there is no pressure on them to disclose more than they wish about their problems. The counsellor must know how to ask the kind of question that will encourage the learner to speak freely – open-ended questions. A counsellor also needs to know how to listen. They must attempt to see things from the learners point of view and must resist the tendency to take over the situation by offering unsolicited advice (however well-intentioned). Counsellors build trust by showing respect, expressing empathy and demonstrating that they are genuine (eg by being prepared to share some of their own personal experience in the area being discussed).

Define an outcome

Outcomes need to be set. The learner has to decide what they want to get out of the counselling process. The more specific the answer, the better.

Describe the problem

The mentor and the learner must understand and be aware of the problem. The learner must talk freely, so the mentor should use open questions to encourage this. The mentor needs to check for emotions and feelings as well as facts. They should be prepared to listen, acknowledge, challenge and summarise. General matters and specific ones should be discussed. In some cases, just airing matters is all that the learner needs to do. When learners freely air their problems, both people can gain a clearer picture of the situation and associated problems.

Understand the problem

The learner should be helped to understand, as fully as possible, why they feel and act as they do given the situation which they have described. People often present negative problems. A mentor should challenge these problems, pushing the individual to make a positive statement on what would improve things.

Make a decision

The learner should be allowed to develop their own solution to the problem. It should be one that suits their own learning style and needs. A number of alternative solutions might be generated and examined. One should then be selected by the learner, and plans made for resourcing and adopting that solution. The interview then needs to be brought to an end, with the counsellor summarising what has been accomplished and what still needs to be done.

USEFUL TIPS

- *Mentors should undergo suitable training to ensure that they have the relevant skills, qualities and attributes.*

- *Formal mentoring schemes require support from senior management and the co-operation of those who supervise those being mentored.*

- *Formal mentoring schemes are most successful when regular reviews are built in. This allows mentors to network and learn from one another. Mentors should help those new to a job or organisation to establish an effective network. Learners become more effective this way, and learn not to be too dependent on their mentors.*

- *Mentors should remember that their behaviour when not mentoring can affect their credibility when they are.*

Quality
approach

part
four

15 Investors in People

This section looks at how Investors In People can help your business.

Introduction

More often than not the quality of the staff you employ determines the success or failure of your business. All too often businesses are unaware of the potential which their existing staff represent. Too many businesses recruit new staff when they identify a skills shortfall, instead of training and developing experienced staff within the business. In recognition of the central role which staff development plays in a business's success, Investors In People was established by the government to encourage employers to take active measures to help them realise the full potential of their workforce. The programme is a useful starting point for any employer wishing to address these issues in their business. Attainment of the National Standard for Effective Investment In People should help your business maintain a professional profile and improve the quality of your overall business operation.

The programme

Investors in People (IiP) is a government funded programme whereby companies make a formal commitment to the training and development of their employees. The programme outlines an action plan for companies to follow, on how to set up a training programme for employees that is linked to the company's objectives. Investors in People is open to all UK businesses regardless of size. Training & Enterprise Councils (TECs) and in Scotland, Local Enterprise Companies (LECs) are responsible for assisting companies to set up IiP programmes. Businesses who would like to implement this programme and achieve the National Standard are offered advice and assistance from their local TEC or LEC. After implementing the programme, a full assessment is conducted at an agreed time by the company and TEC or LEC.

Attainment of the National Standard for Effective Investment In People is intended to demonstrate that a business is committed to staff development; training and development needs are reviewed regularly; specific action is taken to do so; and this process is regularly reviewed and improved.

Getting started

Toolkit

The first step in implementing Investors in People is to contact your local TEC or LEC and ask for the 'Toolkit'. The Toolkit outlines what you will need to do to get started and to carry the whole process through to its conclusion.

Responsible person

Appoint a person to be responsible for managing and overseeing the programme. It is important that someone in the organisation takes responsibility for ensuring the programme is carried out at all levels.

Self-assessment

Carry out a self-assessment of existing provision for training and development in the business. Are staff at all levels trained to do their job? The process should help you to determine exactly what you currently do to train employees as well as where you will need to dedicate more resources. Ultimately the self-assessment will help your company address its business needs and ensure the staff are trained to respond to them.

Written plan

A written plan must be produced. This should include how employees will be trained and developed within the company, and the kind of financial provision you intend to make for this. Your business plan should include job descriptions for all employees.

Produce a portfolio.

When you are ready to be assessed by the local TEC or LEC you will be asked to produce a portfolio. The portfolio should contain your business plan and all written evidence showing how you have implemented IiP. This may include memos, records of discussions with your staff, etc.

Implement the programme.

How you implement your training programme is up to you. Each company is encouraged to adapt its training programme to address the company's needs. Your training programme should address training your employees in the skills they need to be effective in their jobs. This should take into account changes in the company's work environment.

Benefits of Investors in People

Besides increasing company profits, this programme can help businesses in other important areas. Some of the key areas this programme can help a company achieve are as follows:

Improved recruitment

Your business should be better placed to recruit and retain quality staff by making a commitment to develop all its employees. The best candidates should be attracted to a business which shows itself willing to help them learn and advance in their careers. The dedication and loyalty of the workforce should be improved. You should be better able to transfer and/or promote employees within the company rather than seeking new staff.

Improved employee performance

By ensuring every employee has the skills needed to do their job, you will be helping the business achieve its goals. With a proper training programme in place, you can make sure employees adapt better to the changing business environment. Employees who are able to contribute and expand in their careers are more motivated. This can have direct benefits eg decreased employee turnover or absenteeism.

Improved business performance

Improved employee performance will necessarily lead to a more productive and profitable organisation. Fewer problems should arise and the business should be better positioned to move into new products and markets.

Improved reputation

Attainment of the National Standard for Effective Investment In People should help you maintain a professional business profile and therefore act as an endorsement to potential new customers.

Important components

The four principles which the Investors in People programme is based on are as follows:

Commitment

There must be a solid commitment to carry out the programme. A commitment needs to be made from the senior level to front line employees. The company must make an active effort to train new and existing employees. An effective means of demonstrating your business's commitment is by having a written plan and by including staff development as a key element of that plan.

Planning

The business needs to consider in detail just how it will incorporate training into its overall business plan. This will entail linking how employees will be trained to the company's objectives. You should also include targets to be achieved. Ultimately, the aim should be to link employee training to other standards such as National Vocational Qualifications (NVQs).

Action

More important than just having a plan in writing is how you will go about putting it into action. It is important to make real efforts to improve and adapt staff training to meet the needs of the company and its business objectives.

Evaluation

Finally, you need to determine how you will evaluate the effectiveness of the training and development programme. This is achieved mainly by comparing and reviewing a company's written plan to its training targets and goals. Has there been an equal distribution of training for all staff? Do all the employees understand the training policy and their role in achieving company objectives? Has there been an increase or decrease in productivity or turnover?

- *Training and development should include all your employees, even those who are hired on a part-time basis.*

- *Remember that, just as the business adapts to the market, you need to adapt training to meet the needs of the company and its objectives.*

- *For Investors in People to be successful, you will need the support of all your employees from senior level staff to front line employees.*

16 Training for the small business

This section looks at how a small business can provide the appropriate training for its staff.

Introduction

In recent years it has been increasingly recognised that if UK businesses are to be competitive nationally (and internationally) personnel need to be trained to the highest possible levels. Competitive pressures have been reinforced by the prevalence of Total Quality Management methods which, amongst other things, put the emphasis upon staff achieving set standards of competence in their jobs. Training can also help businesses offset the costs related to high staff turnover by helping to retain and develop the people within the organisation. Some believe that small organisations have a greater need for training since staff often have to be more flexible in order to undertake a wide variation of work.

Benefits of training

There are many benefits associated with the development of a training system, some of which are relevant to the individual, some to the organisation.

- The levels of competence amongst the workforce are improved.

- Training is seen as a motivator for staff and may increase job satisfaction.

- Group training sessions can act as a way of developing team spirit.

- Effective training methods ensure that at least minimum standards are achieved.

- With increased interest and awareness of training schemes, an investment in this area may add a competitive edge to the company. In certain cases, qualifications of staff can be cited in advertising material.

- Job flexibility is increased eg improving coverage for absent colleagues and at busy times because staff are trained to a consistent level of competence.

- Receptiveness to new technology can be improved.

- It is cheaper to train existing staff than to recruit pre-trained staff (although this does depend upon the task in question).

- Good standards of staff training are normally equated with a lower staff turnover. People are encouraged to apply to a business which has a reputation for training its staff well.

- Quality is improved and less wastage normally occurs.

- Better trained staff normally improve customer service.

- Training can help you offer career development options for staff within the business. This helps you motivate and retain good employees.

Barriers to training

- It can be expensive to release staff from current tasks in order to allow them to train.

- Lack of in-house expertise and resources is often a problem within small firms.

- It is often difficult to decide who bears the costs of training: the individual, sponsors, the business, or government.

- The degree of training within a company often depends on the ability of managers to identify training needs effectively.

- The choice of appropriate training methods often causes problems for managers and therefore the training effort often proves ineffective.

- Management may see the development of subordinates as a possible threat to their position.

Types of training

There are a number of ways in which employers may train their staff. Each should be evaluated in its own individual context. The most effective strategy usually integrates both formal and informal methods.

Induction

This provides an employee with a general understanding of several basic areas of the business including terms and conditions of employment, company history and activities, office facilities etc. This is particularly valuable to ensure you give new employees statutory information eg health and safety risks etc.

Informal training

Training can be effective on an informal basis. People absorb a great deal of information on the job through general communication, meetings, team briefings, project work etc. This depends very much upon the employee being aware of the learning opportunities around them see Staff Development Methods (section two). Managers may act as trainers through the processes of delegation etc.

On-the-job training

This method of training allows a trainee to observe an experienced worker. The trainee may carry out the job and have an experienced member of staff to ask for help. This method will only be effective if the trainers are well experienced and able to convey the message effectively. There is also the danger that the trainer may have picked up bad habits from their work and may not follow the correct procedures.

Internal/on-site training programmes

This is normally located at a specialist site or area within the company premises. This method of training is sometimes expensive, as it is costly to duplicate some machinery and equipment. This method has the advantage of immediate feedback to the trainees.

External training

This is usually conducted by external trainers and the organisation may feel that they have less control over the training programme. This method may be useful as it introduces new ideas and opinions. Seminars and short courses are frequently advertised and it may be appropriate to send an employee on one. For example, if you wish to develop direct mail promotion, sending an employee on an introductory course will be a good start.

Group training

External trainers are often brought in to give seminars on personal skills such as time management, assertiveness etc. In group training it is important that the training material is relevant to each group member and that the following points are considered:

a) Identify objectives and make sure that they are clear to the group.

b) Praise members if they achieve a goal or good performance.

c) Make the lecture material interesting and the delivery of it lively.

d) Avoid excessive use of jargon.

c) Open learning packages

These usually include written material and visual aids. However, the employee must be self-motivated to work. Employees can benefit from an independent mentor (inside or outside the company) to help them evaluate their progress.

Professional training

Many of your employees will be seeking to advance their careers by undertaking part-time courses in order to achieve professional qualifications. Qualifications may be quite specifically vocational eg accountancy, total quality management diploma, printing industry qualifications etc. Others may be of a more general nature eg Master in Business Administration, Diploma in Management Studies. Many employers are ambivalent about how they should treat such activities. It is good to encourage staff to improve themselves, but on the other hand, if they leave, others could benefit from your investment. Develop criteria about how to treat any applications for support or time off eg relevance to job, organisation, development potential of the individual etc. Have a policy eg if staff leave within say two years of qualifying, they must refund part or all of the employer's contribution to their training.

Assessing training needs

In determining training needs the situation may be assessed at a number of levels.

The entire firm

a) Is the workforce size increasing?

b) Current job flexibility situation.

c) Introduction of new technology.

d) Diversification.

e) Costs.

A carefully thought through programme of training for the whole business, and for key employees, will often be necessary for a business wishing to implement the ISO 9000 quality system. Professional qualifications, together with staff seminars, are a good way to promote the new ideas which it is necessary to introduce. Organisations undergoing cultural change, or other traumatic events such as mergers will find a company wide training programme useful. Some businesses choose to review all training needs on an annual basis. This is often known as a Training Needs Analysis.

Individual departments

Is it cost effective if wider training areas are covered for individual departments? If one department tends to budget for more training than another this can be divisive.

Individual training

Individual learning methods and their effectiveness vary, but some basic guidelines are often useful as a starting point:

a) Learning tends to be more effective when the trainee is involved rather than just observing.

b) Active learning seems to be more productive than passive.

c) Employees tend to learn more when training is put into context relevant to their work.

Forward planning

It is also advisable and increasingly common for trainers to look forward to anticipate the future by trying to assess how the person's job is likely to change. This involves the consideration of various points:

a) What is likely to change within a person's job description?

b) What are the output objectives for the near future?

c) What current methods of performance appraisal are used?

Evaluation

Training can be expensive so if a company is to invest in a training programme it is important that the benefits are assessed. An important part of evaluation is feedback from trainees. In accepting this feedback it is important that

- The trainee is honest.

- The trainer does not defend criticism before asking why it has been made and assessing whether or not he/she feels that it is justified.

- The trainer raises probing questions to expand and clarify feedback.

The outcome of training programmes should be evaluated in relation to all relevant areas of the business in order to get a realistic assessment. This may involve linking the outcome to the overall objectives of the company, department or individual.

USEFUL TIPS

● *Develop a policy which outlines your approach to training your staff. Co-ordinate and plan training activities as part of your business planning process. Build the cost of training into your budgets.*

● *Make sure that everyone in authority understands the benefits and is committed to training the workforce to the appropriate level. If training initiatives are only a token effort, this can be counter-productive. Expectations will have been raised and not fulfilled.*

● *Make someone responsible for implementing training programmes. If the person you appoint has the correct expertise this will help the business achieve*

professional standards and source any
funding which might be available.

● *Seek advice from your Training and*
Enterprise Council (Local Enterprise
Company in Scotland) on training for
your staff and funding to support your
training activities. Ask your TEC for
information on the Investors in People
programme.

17 National Vocational Qualifications

This section explains the National Vocational Qualifications system.

Introduction

Vocational training and education, as opposed to general education, give people the skills and knowledge to carry out particular types of work. Courses and qualifications are run by hundreds of different organisations around the UK covering anything from furniture production to marine craft fitting. For employers and employees alike choosing and evaluating vocational courses can be a difficult task.

National Vocational Qualifications (NVQ) or Scottish Vocational Qualifications (SVQ) were designed to reform the somewhat confused state of vocational qualifications in the United Kingdom and bring them into a new structured framework where individuals can progress towards qualifications at their own pace. NVQs are based on national standards and are designed to address the future labour and training needs of UK industry. They can be studied whilst working in all types and sizes of organisations. Individuals can work towards NVQs whilst in paid or unpaid employment, at college or in their own time. NVQs are suitable for people in work, those returning to work and school or college leavers.

The National Council for Vocational Qualifications (NCVQ)

This body was set up in October 1986 by the Government and was responsible for establishing the NVQ framework of qualifications. The NCVQ does not award the qualifications itself. It is an overall body which approves vocational qualifications and makes sure that the different NVQs are comparable in standard and are of the right quality. The NCVQ should ensure that qualifications enable workers to achieve standards that allow them and their companies to perform well in the world markets. There should be no discrimination of any kind. NVQs should be accessible to all, regardless of gender, age and race. The NCVQ is also responsible for the recent development of the new General National Vocational Qualifications (GNVQ).

Awarding/lead bodies

The awarding or lead bodies set the standards and competences that the NVQs and SVQs are based on. There are different types of lead bodies; those that are existing training boards but take on the NVQs as well, a consortium made up of a few lead bodies in similar areas and others created to determine standards that cover a wide range of employment issues. The lead bodies identify the competences needed in a particular industry to carry out the work. They decide on the units and the qualification. Many of the awarding bodies are quite small but three awarding bodies, BTEC, City and Guilds and the RSA provide most vocational qualifications. Some NVQs will have more than one awarding body for example the NVQ in Business Administration has five awarding bodies; City and Guilds, London Chamber of Commerce and Industry, BTEC, Pitman and RSA. An individual wanting to take this NVQ will have to choose which awarding body they want.

Subject areas

NVQs cover most subject areas and are suitable for people wanting to work in the service sector, as well as manufacturing and heavy industry. They are grouped into 11 broad sections:

- Tending animals, plants and land

- Extracting and providing natural resources

- Construction

- Engineering

- Manufacturing

- Transport

- Providing goods and services

- Providing health, social care and protective services

- Providing business services

- Communication

- Developing and extending knowledge and skills.

Within these areas a wide variety of subjects can be studied including, for example, commercial horticulture, sea fishing, carpentry and joinery, footwear repair, steelmaking, beauty therapy, dry cleaning, purchasing, book design etc. Not all subjects are available yet at all levels.

A national database of vocational qualifications is available which gives details of all available NVQs including all the units within each one and the required criteria. This database will help to provide information on training and career progression for individuals and companies. It is held on a subscription basis and will be held in some TECs, career centres and companies etc.

Levels

Although they are not assessing the same types of things, an NVQ level 2 equates roughly to four GCSEs and an NVQ Level 3 equates to two A levels. A person can decide at which level they want to enter the NVQ system. They do not have to start at the lowest level. There are five levels of competence in NVQs. Some general guidelines on the difficulty of the levels are as follows:

Level 1: Foundation level where competence must be shown in basic and often routine activities.

Level 2: Competence in a broader range of work some of which involves non-routine tasks.

Level 3: Competence in various skill activities including some complex and supervisory tasks.

Level 4: Competence in a wide range of activities perhaps with managerial responsibility.

Level 5: Competence in more complex tasks with a large amount of personal autonomy, planning, evaluation etc, and often major responsibility for others.

Each NVQ consists of a number of separate units within which there are standards that must be attained. A person gets credit for each unit completed. People can choose some options within the NVQ. The units completed are shown on the individual's certificate which provides a full record of achievement.

Assessment

NVQs are available in modular form. There are no examinations as such. NVQ assessment takes a variety of forms including practical tests as well as projects and written work. Assessment depends on the type of the NVQ which is being worked for. Practical competence is important as is work based assessment. The work is marked and the person is said to be competent or not competent in the NVQ taken. No credits or distinctions are awarded. NVQs offer more flexibility as individuals can decide at what level they want to start. There are no time limits on completion. NVQs are awarded for being competent at carrying out a job to the required standards and not just the ability to pass exams. If a person can already do the job to the required standard they can get a credit for that.

The Accreditation of Prior Learning (APL) means that past work experience and competence can count towards NVQs. The worker can put together a portfolio giving examples of their capabilities, for example documents, photographs, references etc. Certificates are awarded showing the credits that an individual has achieved. A person has their own record, the National Record of Achievement (NRA) providing the person with a personal record of their training. The National Record means that employers and staff can plan the training to benefit both the company and the individual. People with learning difficulties can get credits even if they may not be able to earn a full NVQ.

General National Vocational Qualifications (GNVQ)

These qualifications have been introduced recently to form more vocational qualifications for those pupils who want to stay on in full-time education at school or sixth form college after the age of 16. They are seen as a practical alternative to 'A' levels for work related qualifications. They should help to prepare the students for work as well as higher education. GNVQs will be in modular form and allow students to progress at their own rate. They were widely available from September 1993. There are three levels to GNVQs:

Level 1:   Foundation

Level 2:   Intermediate

Level 3:   Advanced

Benefits to employers

A business needs products or services to be of a high quality and this depends very much upon the abilities of the people they employ. If staff are trained properly then they can achieve their full potential and so do their job more effectively. Motivation is also improved. NVQs are set by the lead bodies from industry so they should match the needs of the employer and represent their interests in that particular area. It is essential that the skills of the workers match the needs of industry and NVQs are intended to be as relevant as possible to the realities of working life. The training needs of the staff can be properly identified and it is easier to assess the abilities of prospective employees and select the right new members of staff. Many larger companies are encouraging their staff to work towards NVQs. The qualifications are suitable for all levels of staff.

Benefits to employees

When applying for a new job it is easy for the prospective employer to know the level of achievement of a candidate. NVQs show that a candidate is capable of doing the job as the assessment is practical and work based. You have your own record of achievement showing all the elements that you have reached. NVQs allow an individual to have a career break and not miss out on completing their qualifications and some past work experience can count towards these new qualifications.

USEFUL TIPS

● *Check that the courses you and your staff choose have NVQ status or are working towards it. Encourage your lead body to go down this route.*

● *Contact your local Training and Enterprise Council (Local Enterprise Company in Scotland) for details of NVQs available in your particular industry sector.*

● *Ask your TEC/LEC about Investors in People which will help you develop ways to evaluate training needs in your business.*

18 Business and management courses

This section gives an overview of the main types of business and management courses available.

Introduction

Whilst certain types of people are better at running a business than others, training in management and business skills will normally improve the ability of the owner manager to put their qualities to best use. Short courses will allow you to acquire practical skills whilst running your business. A course of full-time study will provide a much more in-depth understanding of how business and management works. With the right balance of knowledge and practical experience, strategic decisions and the management of staff should be much improved.

Enterprise training

Short training programmes are available for people starting a business. Programmes are sponsored by Training and Enterprise Councils (Local Enterprise Companies in Scotland) and will appear in various forms, with various names, depending upon the approach adopted by the local TEC or LEC. Programmes may be divided into three main areas:

- Courses for those starting up a business (normally provided in the form of Training for Work programmes).

- Evening seminars for people in work who wish to start a business.

- Seminars for people who have recently established their own business.

For the most part, training is available as a series of one or two day seminars. Depending upon experience and need, participants may do only a selection of the seminars on offer. Seminar topics include marketing, pricing, advertising and promotion, direct marketing, personal selling skills, customer care, export marketing, book-keeping, understanding finance, accounting with computers, taxation, effective management, employing people, time/stress/crisis management, computers in business. Small business seminars are a well established means to make concise relevant training available as and when it is required. Contact your local TEC/LEC to find out which courses are available and what the entry requirements are.

National Vocational Qualifications

Vocational courses allow people to acquire skills and knowledge for particular professions, trades and other specific jobs. Vocational courses are being standardised and vetted by the National Council for Vocational Qualifications. The NCVQ is establishing the National Vocational Qualifications (NVQ) network. The NCVQ does not award qualifications itself, but approves or 'accredits' them.

If you are seeking a vocational qualification in business or management, make sure the course you choose leads to an NVQ. The NVQ in Business Administration, for example, can be offered in-house for employees or in colleges and training organisations. Level 1 has a core of units with a choice of either administrative, financial or secretarial specialism at level 2. Assessment is usually by practical demonstration in the workplace. Candidates keep a full log of their activities with examples and evidence of tasks completed. The NVQ in Business Administration is available at three levels. City and Guilds is one of the UK's leading awarding bodies for vocational qualifications and can provide further details about where courses can be provided around the UK. You can also gain NVQs through Accreditation of Prior Learning where an assessment of your existing skills and experience is carried out.

Business and Technology Education Council (BTEC)

BTEC Diplomas and Certificates usually reach a level lower than that required for the award of a degree. There is usually a carefully defined course in a specialised or vocational subject lasting one or two years. BTEC offer nationally recognised qualifications in a wide range of business and finance subjects and are usually studied with a view to a particular vocation. In Scotland similar qualifications are administered by the Scottish Vocational Education Council (SCOTVEC). A common business course is the BTEC in Business and Finance.

BTEC First Diploma in Business and Finance

This course is for those who wish to follow careers as juniors or trainees in business and commerce. Each course contains four compulsory subjects and four optional subjects. The Business World looks at how organisations are structured and how they work. Administrative Systems looks at information management and communication skills. Business Resources and Procedures covers physical and human resources. People in Business covers the role of people in organisations including the rights and responsibilities between employers and employees. Additional options vary and may include business information technology, customer care, European business and production.

BTEC National in Business and Finance

National awards are equivalent to 'A' level standard. All the BTEC national courses contain Working in Organisations, made up of eight compulsory subjects plus options. There are four optional subjects in the National Certificate and eight in the National Diploma. Core subjects include business structure and goals, business environment, marketing process, physical resources, financial resources, human resources, administrative systems and innovation and change. Options can include areas such as business european studies, international trade, sales and small business enterprise.

BTEC Higher National in Business and Finance

Higher National awards approach degree standard. The course begins with a foundation programme and culminates in an assignment drawing from five core subjects. Core subjects in year one include management of human resources, finance business environment, business law and statistics for business application. An additional option of either marketing or finance is then taken. Year two continues the core subjects of management of human resources, finance and the business environment. Options include advanced accounting, business taxation, information systems, logistics, purchasing, marketing communications, personnel management and total quality management.

Other higher diplomas and certificates

Many other business and management courses are available at the higher level. For example, the BTEC Certificate in Management Studies (CMS) aims to provide a basic introduction to the functional areas involved in management. Course components include what is management?, managing people, managing money, communications and managing operations.

College diplomas and certificates

A few colleges and universities offer their own certificate or diploma level courses. For example, the University of Northumbria at Newcastle offer their own diploma in marketing which leads to the Diploma of the Chartered Institute of Marketing. Modules include basic marketing, the marketing environment, marketing communications (creative aspects and media planning), marketing research (methods and techniques), marketing strategy and planning, and international marketing. Some college courses may not be validated by a recognised validating body such as BTEC.

First degrees

University degrees consist of at least three years full-time study with the student having obtained the necessary entry qualifications. General business courses include business studies, economics and commerce. More specialised degrees include accounting and business information technology. The most well known first degree course is probably Business Studies. Courses are usually over four years with one year's work placement in industry, either undertaken in the third year or split over two periods. Courses can vary between universities. The first year usually aims to give a basic grounding, covering a wide range of subjects including accounting, marketing, quantitative methods, organisational behaviour, information technology, business law and economics. The second year usually consists of a wider range of 'electives' allowing students to specialise. Final year students usually specialise in one of about six or seven main areas including marketing, human resource management, finance, law, business economics and operations management.

Higher degrees

Masters degrees

Masters courses are usually studied on completion of a first degree. Subjects can include economics, international business, business administration and business strategy. For example, the MSc in Finance at the London Business School has a vocational bias, is practically based and can be studied part-time over two years, mostly in the evenings. Core subjects include financial accounting, financial accounting and analysis, corporate finance and capital markets. Electives are then chosen as well as an international financial centre field project. The MSc is designed for experienced managers and finance professionals in industry, commerce and the City.

Master in Business Administration

The MBA is an internationally recognised postgraduate, post-experience qualification intended to prepare individuals for middle and senior management. Most MBA courses offer a range of core subjects which include accounting and finance, operations management, business policy, economics, human resource management, marketing, information systems and strategic planning. Electives may include topics such as capital markets, business in Europe and strategic marketing. Students also have to do a dissertation of about 25,000 words.

Postgraduate diplomas and certificates

A number of courses for graduates are offered in universities, including short specialist courses in Management and Business Studies. For example, the Diploma in Management Studies can be studied full or part time. Year one might include management effectiveness, understanding financial management, managing people, management information organising management and organising work. Year two could cover management analysis, environmental management, small business simulation for managers and managing strategy. Students also have to complete a research project.

Open University qualifications

The OU requires no formal qualifications for admission to first degree courses. Courses are studied independently, usually at home, with support from a network of tutors and counsellors. There is a fee for each course. Business and management courses are taught at Certificate, Diploma and MBA level. The Open University Business School (OBS) offers courses leading to professional management qualifications or just on one or two courses to develop specific skills.

- The Professional Certificate in Management includes The Capable Manager, The Effective Manager, Accounting for Managers, Accounting and the PC for Managers and Managing Customer and Client Relations.

- The Professional Diploma in Management includes Managing Development and Change, Managing Resources for the Market, Planning and Managing Change, Managing in the Competitive Environment, Retail Management, and Project Management.

- MBA is studied in two stages. Stage 1 can be completed either by one intensive nine month course or by completing the professional Certificate and Diploma in Management. Stage two comprises a compulsory course and options.

- The OBS also provides a range of courses designed for owners and managers of small and medium-sized enterprises including the Certificate in Small Business Management and Women in Management.

Professional institutions and associations

Many institutes and associations also provide a range of recognised professional and vocational qualifications in the fields of Business and Management Studies. For example, the Institute of Commercial Management offers a Diploma in Business Studies and also a Graduate Diploma in Management Studies. The Chartered Association of Certified Accountants runs the Diploma in Accounting and Finance. The course involves four areas of study; financial accounting, principles of management, financial management and management accounting. Diploma holders can, after payment of a fee to the association, use the designating letters CDipAF.

USEFUL TIPS

- *Introduce systems to ensure that all your staff's training needs are reviewed and addressed on a regular basis.*

- *Contact the relevant course providers direct for up to date details of courses and entry requirements.*

- *Local TECs/LECs will help you identify suitable courses and any funding available.*

Appendices

part
five

five

19 **Further reading**

Section 1

Creating Top Flight Teams, Hilarie Owen,
Kogan Page, 1996

*Superteams: A Blueprint for Organisational
Success*, Colin Hastings, Peter Bixby,
Rani Chaudhry-Lawton, William Collins Sons
& Co. Ltd, 1988

A Handbook of Structured Experiences,
J William Pfeiffer, University Associates, 1985

*Management Teams: Why They
Succeed or Fail*, R. Meredith Belbin,
William Heinemann Ltd, 1981

Section 2

Introducing Investors in People,
Mary McLuskey, Kogan Page, 1996

*Managing Change through Training and
Development*, Jim Stewart, Kogan Page, 1996

Section 3

Effective Negotiating, Colin Robinson,
Kogan Page, 1996

The Language of Negotiation,
Joan Mulholland, Routledge, 1991

Successful Negotiating in a Week,
Peter Fleming, Institute of Management

Negotiating: Everybody Wins, Vanessa Helps,
BBC Publications, 1992

Section 4

Assertiveness at Work, Kate and Ken Back,
McGraw-Hill, 1992

*Putting Assertiveness to Work:
A Programme for Management Excellence*,
Graham Willcocks and Steve Morris,
Pitman Publishing, 1996

Section 5

Managing Quality for the First Time,
D Cranswick, Pitman Publishing, 1996

Time is Money: Save It, Lothar J Seiwert,
Kogan Page, 1991

*How to Get Control of Your
Time and Your Life*, Alan Lakein, Gower, 1985

Section 6

The Handbook of Communication Skills,
B Hurst, Kogan Page, 1996

*Improving Your Presentation Skills:
A Complete Action Kit*, Michael Stevens,
Kogan Page 1989

High Impact Presentation Skills Workshop,
P Ittner & A Douds, Kogan Page, 1989

Section 7

Managing Stress, David Fontana,
British Psychological Society, 1989

*Managing Stress: Emotion and Power at
Work*, Tim Newton, Sage, 1995

Managing Stress: Keeping Calm Under Fire,
Barbara Braham Irwin, 1994

Pressure at Work, T Arroba and K James,
McGraw Hill, 1992

Coping with Stress, H Greenberg,
Prentice Hall, 1980

Section 8

Report Writing Skills, Roy Jeffs,
Oliver and Boyd, 1990

Report Writing, J Van Emden and J Easteal,
McGraw Hill, 2nd ed, 1993

Professional Report Writing, Simon Mort,
Gower, 1992

How to Write a Report – A Step by Step Guide to Effective Report Writing, How to Books, 3rd ed, 1996

Section 9

Planning to Succeed in Business, David Irwin, Pitman, 1995

A Practical Guide to Project Planning, C. Burton and N. Michael, Kogan Page, 1994

Section 10

Planning to Succeed in Business, David Irwin, Pitman, 1995

Problem Solving and Decision Making, Graham Wilson, Kogan Page, 1993

Practical Problem Solving For Managers, Michael Stephens, Kogan Page, 1988

Effective Decision Making – A Practical Guide for Management, Helga Drummond, Kogan Page, 1993

Managing People for the First Time, Peter Stannack, Pitman, 1993

Section 11

Management Guide to Delegating, Kate Keenan, Ravette, 1996

Delegating Authority, Andrew Schwarz, Cassell, 1995

Delegation Skills, Bruce Tepper, Irwin, 1994

Section 12

How to Hold Better Meetings, Alan Barker, Kogan Page, 1997

Effective Meetings, Maria Pemberton, Industrial Society, 1990

Effective Meeting Skills, Marion Haynes, Kogan Page, 1988

Make Meetings Work, Lifeskills Communication Ltd, 1991

Meetings, Howell Parry, Croner Publications, 1991

Section 13

Managing People for the First Time, Peter Stannack, Pitman, 1993

Leadership: The Art Of Motivation, Nick Thornley and Dan Lees, Century Business, 1993

How to be an Even Better Manager, Michael Armstrong, Kogan Page, 1994

How to Solve your People Problems,
Jane Allan, Kogan Page, 1989

How to Manage People at Work –
a Practical Guide to Effective Leadership,
John Humphries, How to Books, 1995

Section 14

The Mentoring Manager, Gareth Lewis,
Pitman, 1996

Mentoring, Reg Hamilton,
Industrial Society, 1993

Section 15

Your local TEC or LEC will provide you with
free information about Investors in People
– see next section

Section 16

Managing People For the First Time,
Peter Stannack, Pitman, 1993

Training for the Small Business,
J Barnett and L Graham, Kogan Page, 1992

Successful Training Practice – A Manager's
Guide to Personnel Development,
A H Anderson, Blackwell Business, 1993

Section 17

British Qualifications, Kogan Page
(annual publication)

Training Your Staff, Industrial Society

*Planning and Implementing Your NVQ
System*, Shirley Fletcher, Kogan Page, 1997

*European Vocational Education and Training
Systems: A Guide to Vocational Education
and Training in the European Community*,
Helen Collins, Kogan Page, 1993

20 Useful addresses

Addresses and telephone numbers for your local **Business Link, Training and Enterprise Council** (**Local Enterprise Company** in Scotland) and **Local Enterprise Agency** may be found in your telephone directory.

The **Business Link Signpost** service on (0345) 567 765 can put you in touch with your nearest Business Link office. Local **Scottish Business Shops** can be contacted on (0141) 248 6014 or (0800) 787 878 for callers from Scotland. For **Business Connect** in Wales call (0345) 969 798. **Local Enterprise Development Unit** (LEDU) in Northern Ireland can be contacted on (01232) 491 031.

The **National Federation of Enterprise Agencies** can put you in touch with your nearest agency. Ring them on 01234 354055 or on the internet at http://www.pne.org/cobweb/nfea

Institute of Personnel and Development
IPD House, 35 Camp Road
Wimbledon, London SW19 4UX
Tel: (0181) 971 9000

Industrial Society
Small Business Department
Robert Hyde House, 48 Bryanston Square
London W1H 7LN
Tel: (0171) 262 2401

Employment Department
Moorfoot, Sheffield S1 4PQ
Tel: (01742) 753275

Scottish Enterprise
120 Bothwell Street
Glasgow G2 7JP
Tel: (0141) 248 2700

**Training Enterprise and
Education Directorate**
Moorfoot, Sheffield
South Yorkshire S1 4PQ
Tel: (01742) 753275

Vocational Educational Unit
City & Guilds of London Institute
46 Britannia Street
London WC1X 9RG
Tel: (0171) 278 2468

**Business and Technology
Education Council (BTEC)**
Central House
Upper Woburn Place
London WC1H OHH
Tel: (0171) 413 8400

Scottish Vocational Education Council (SCOTVEC)
Hanover House
24 Douglas Street
Glasgow G2 7NQ
Tel: (0141) 248 7900

National Council for Vocational Qualifications (NCVQ)
222 Euston Road
London NW1 2BZ
Tel: (0171) 387 9898

City and Guilds of London Institute
76 Portland Place
London WIN 4AA
Tel: (0171) 278 2468

RSA Examinations Board
Westwood Way
Coventry CV4 8HS
Tel: (01203) 470033

The Open University
Walton Hall
Milton Keynes MK7 6YY
Tel: (01908) 653028

Index

Hawksmere – focused on helping you improve your performance

Hawksmere plc is one of the UK's foremost training organisations. We design and present more than 450 public seminars a year, in the UK and internationally, for professionals and executives in business, industry and the public sector, in addition to a comprehensive programme of specially tailored in-company courses. Every year, well over 15,000 people attend a Hawksmere programme. The companies which use our programmes and the number of courses we successfully repeat reflect our reputation for uncompromising quality.

Our policy is to continually re-examine and develop our programmes, updating and improving them. Our aim is to anticipate the shifting and often complex challenges facing everyone in business and the professions and to provide programmes of high quality, focused on producing practical results – helping you improve your performance.

Our objective for each delegate

At Hawksmere we have one major aim – that every delegate leaves each programme better equipped to put enhanced techniques and expertise to practical use. All our speakers are practitioners who are experts in their own field: as a result, the information and advice on offer at a Hawksmere programme is expert and tried and tested, practical yet up-to-the-minute.

Our programmes span all levels, from introductory skills to sophisticated techniques and the implications of complex legislation. Reflecting their different aims and objectives, they also vary in format from one day multi-speaker conferences to one and two day seminars, three day courses and week long residential workshops.

For a brochure on any particular area of interest or for more information generally, please call Hawksmere Customer Services on 0171 824 8257 or fax on 0171 730 4293.

Hawksmere In-company Training

In addition to its public seminars Hawksmere works with client companies developing and delivering a wide range of tailored training in industries as diverse as retailing, pharmaceuticals, public relations, engineering and service industries such as banking and insurance – the list is long.

We specialise in a wide range of personnel topics including Personnel and Employment Law, Competencies, Empowerment, Coaching, Appraisal, Interviewing, Communication and Motivation.

The Hawksmere In-Company team is headed by Aileen Clark, who has worked extensively in management training and development for the past twenty years, building successful courses for a wide range of businesses in both the public and private sectors. Call Aileen or her team on 0171 824 8257 for expert advice on your training needs without any obligation.

Thorogood: the publishing business of the Hawksmere Group

Thorogood publishes a wide range of books, reports, special briefings, psychometric tests and videos.

Listed below is a selection of key titles.

Masters in Management

Mastering business planning and strategy
Paul Elkin £19.95

Mastering financial management
Stephen Brookson £19.95

Mastering leadership
Michael Williams £19.95

Mastering negotiations
Eric Evans £19.95

Mastering people management
Mark Thomas £19.95

Mastering project management
Cathy Lake £19.95

The Essential Guides

The essential guide to buying
and selling unquoted businesses
Ian Smith £25

The essential guide to business
planning and raising finance
Naomi Langford-Wood & Brian Salter £25

The essential business guide to the Internet
Naomi Langford-Wood & Brian Salter £19.95

Other titles

The John Adair handbook of management
and leadership – *edited by Neil Thomas*
£19.95

The handbook of management fads
Steve Morris £8.95

The inside track to successful management
Dr Gerald Kushel £16.95

The pension trustee's handbook (2nd edition)
Robin Ellison £25

Reports and Special Briefings

Dynamic budgetary control
David Allen £95

Evaluating and monitoring strategies
David Allen £95

Software licence agreements
Robert Bond £125

Negotiation tactics for software and hi-tech
agreements – *Robert Bond* £165

Achieving business excellence, quality and
performance improvement
Colin Chapman and Dennis Hopper   £95

Employment law aspects of mergers
and acquisitions – *Michael Ryley*   £125

Techniques for successful
management buy-outs – *Ian Smith*   £125

Financial techniques for business
acquisitions and disposals – *Ian Smith*   £125

Techniques for minimising the risks of
acquisitions: commercial due diligence
Ian Smith & Kevin Jewell   £125

Mergers and acquisitions – confronting
the organisation and people issue
Mark Thomas   £125

An employer's guide to the management of
complaints of sex and race discrimination
Christopher Walter   £125

Securing business funding from
Europe and the UK – *Peter Wilding*   £125

Influencing the European Union
Peter Wilding   £125

Standard conditions of commercial contract
Peter Wilding   £139

To order any title, or to request more information,
please call Thorogood Customer Services on
0171 824 8257 or fax on 0171 730 4293.